"This is one of the most practical book. It is also one of the most profound."

Peter Kreeft, profe~~s~~
and Kin
including
and *Jacob's Ladder* ~~...~~

"This is not just another apologetics book. *How to Talk to a Skeptic* is a compelling synthesis of worldview training, Bible teaching, and practical discussion tips. You don't have to be a philosophy student to use it; believers in all walks of life will benefit from Johnson's help to answer skeptics with truth, gentleness, and respect. He shows how vestiges of bad theology end up maligning the character of God causing skepticism for the nonbeliever, and why good theology is important in the task of conversational evangelism. The insights on how to ask good questions and frame evangelistic dialogue are refreshing and are born from Johnson's many years of experience with Christianity's critics. This is a significant book; it uniquely probes important questions that are usually left behind in the apologetics discussions. I encourage you to read it!"

Rick Schenker, president, Ratio Christi

"Don Johnson has been making the case for Christianity for many years now here in Southern California. As a skeptic and 'late-believer' myself, I am grateful that Don has carefully crafted a book that will help believers understand the issues, frame their discussions, and intelligently interact with nonbelievers in their midst. Don uses many personal examples and has created a resource that is accessible, informative, and engaging."

J. Warner Wallace, cold case detective, Christian case maker
at Stand to Reason, and author of *Cold-Case Christianity:
A Homicide Detective Investigates the Claims of the Gospels*

"Don Johnson's new book, *How to Talk to a Skeptic*, provides a much-needed resource for people who are intimidated by sharing their faith with perceived intellectuals. It's easy to feel inadequate when others seem so confident, and we think of the perfect response an hour after the conversation ends. This book doesn't just provide a list of catch phrases and points to make in a discussion. Instead, it's about how to build a genuine relationship with a person of non-faith, using a caring approach to open an honest interaction about faith. It's one of the few books that doesn't see the skeptic as the enemy."

Mike Bechtle, author, *Evangelism for the Rest of Us:
Sharing Christ Within Your Personality Style*
and *Confident Conversation: How to Communicate
Effectively in Any Situation*

"When the majority of what is on offer for reaching skeptics reduces to a wooden 'paint-by-numbers' sort of evangelism, Donald Johnson has proposed a fresh and conversational approach. Unlike most evangelistic strategies, the success of Donald Johnson's method is clear to anyone who has heard the countless discussions he has had with skeptics on his radio show. Rather than trying to sell Christian theism to skeptics as a product, Donald Johnson offers an approach that organically demonstrates the truth of the Christian worldview."

Braxton Hunter, professor of apologetics at Trinity College and Seminary, president of the Conference of Southern Baptist Evangelists, and the director of evangelism and apologetics for Trinity Crusades for Christ

"*How to Talk to a Skeptic* is both practical and accessible. Don Johnson has done the American church in the twenty-first century a service by helping us think about how to engage unbelievers with truth and grace."

Paul Schliep, director of Credentialing and Theological Health for Evangelical Free Church of America West Region

"Don Johnson has combined a deep knowledge of apologetics with practical advice on how to actually discuss Christianity with skeptics. This impressive book combines clear thinking, good writing, and apologetics zeal. Bravo!"

Douglas Groothuis, professor of philosophy, Denver Seminary, head of the Apologetics and Ethics Master's Degree Program, and author of *Christian Apologetics*

"*How to Talk to a Skeptic* will bring real encouragement to all who seek to share the good news with nonbelievers, but instead find themselves getting bogged down in a swamp of objections. That's because Don Johnson clearly shows how we must establish the contextual ground rules before we can engage in fruitful discussions about ultimate reality. *How to Talk to a Skeptic* makes the indispensable point that Christianity is not a product to be sold but a comprehensive and intelligent worldview to be embraced. This is a great book."

Stan Guthrie, president, Stan Guthrie Communications, coauthor, *The Sacrament of Evangelism*, author, *All That Jesus Asks*, and editor-at-large, *Christianity Today*

"I've been involved in apologetics and worldview ministries since the '70s, and I'm always looking for material that will help my students and fellow-believers. Not only do I want them to get the facts about the evidence for the Christian faith but also understand how to communicate those ideas in a winsome way that will move skeptics to want to honestly seek out why the gospel is relevant to them. Don Johnson has given us one of those books. I plan to recommend it to my students and to my skeptical friends."

Randy Rodden, president, Answers International Ministries, professor of philosophy and religion, Community Christian College, teaching pastor, Valley of the Falls Community Church, Forest Falls, CA

How to Talk to a
Skeptic

How to Talk to a
Skeptic

An **Easy-to-Follow Guide** for
Natural Conversations and Effective Apologetics

Donald J. Johnson

BETHANY HOUSE PUBLISHERS
a division of Baker Publishing Group
Minneapolis, Minnesota

© 2013 by Donald J. Johnson

Published by Bethany House Publishers
11400 Hampshire Avenue South
Bloomington, Minnesota 55438
www.bethanyhouse.com

Bethany House Publishers is a division of
Baker Publishing Group, Grand Rapids, Michigan

Printed in the United States of America

Library of Congress Cataloging-in-Publication Data is on file at the Library of Congress, Washington, DC.

ISBN 978-0-7642-1122-5 (pbk.)

Cover design by Dan Pitts

Author is represented by D. C. Jacobson & Associates, LLC.

13 14 15 16 17 18 19   7 6 5 4 3 2 1

For my amazing wife, Kendra

Contents

Introduction: How to Reach a Culture of Radical
Unbelief   11

Part One: A Framework for Fruitful Conversations

1. No Selling Required   19
2. The Big Picture   31
3. The State of the Doubter's Knowledge   45

Part Two: What Skeptics Need to Know About God

4. Love and the Meaning of Life   53
5. The Reason for the Rules   73
6. What Jesus Meant by That Whole "Born Again"
   Thing   87
7. Why Hell Is Fair and Heaven Won't Be Boring   105
8. How to Think About the Bible   123

Part Three: Dealing With the Data

9. The God Hypothesis   149
10. Christianity and Pagan Myths   167

Contents

11. The World Is Not Enough   187
12. Up Close and Personal With God   207
13. Hypocrisy, Sex, and Other Causes of Skepticism   231
14. Telling the World Its Story   253

Notes   255

/////////// Introduction

How to Reach a Culture of Radical Unbelief

On March 3, 2005, *The Washington Times* published an article about the decline of atheism.[1] The author presented several good reasons to believe that godlessness was in trouble and there would be fewer atheists in the future. I distinctly remember the piece because I heartily endorsed its thesis on my radio show that week. Boy was I wrong! While the *Times* certainly presented solid reasons for people to reject atheism,[2] the prognosis that more people actually were going to do so was clearly premature. Atheism, at least in America, is in ascension, not decline, as more and more people openly reject the existence of God.[3]

This trend is largely due to the work of a few vocal and aggressive atheist writers, the most popular of whom are Sam Harris, Christopher Hitchens, Richard Dawkins, and Daniel Dennett. Inspired by the terrorist attacks of 9/11,[4] the "Four Horsemen" of the new atheism have sold millions of books railing not only against Islam, but religion in general. Along with Hollywood types like Bill Maher, they have made atheism fashionable, particularly among college students.

This movement is part of a larger cultural shift toward religious skepticism in general. While not all skeptics embrace an ardent form of atheism, they all are becoming much more cynical about traditional religion and openly suspicious of any strong claims to revealed truth. As this culture of radical doubt has gained strength, my email inbox has been inundated with requests for help in dealing with it. Christians are running into more and more friends, family members, and co-workers who not only question the faith, but are antagonistic toward it, and they aren't sure how to interact with them.

There are three main areas in which people request assistance.

First, many people want to know how to respond to challenges to Christianity. They are looking for answers to tough questions and rebuttals for difficult arguments. For example, Tim sent me this email:

Hi, Don,

An old friend from high school has looked me up on Facebook. He has abandoned his faith and is an aggressive atheist. He keeps trying to negate my faith, so I've been asking him to come up with something besides just telling me I'm stupid. Finally today he sent a list of supposed errors in the Bible. I am no expert on different manuscripts but . . . Junias the female apostle given a sex change? What? I don't see anything in the Bible about this—am I missing something? If I can trouble you for some input . . .

Tyler was also looking for answers, although in a more general sense:

Dear Don,

I will be beginning my freshman year at a secular college, studying civil engineering, in about a month. I have been reading books such as *Reasonable Faith*, *Tactics*, and *Evidence for the Resurrection* and listening to your podcasts and others like *Stand to Reason* and apologetics.com for the last year. I am not sure what I will be facing at college, so I wanted to know if there was anything that you know of that would help me with these challenges. Is there a group of things that I should memorize in order to be prepared, or any books/podcasts that I should study both during and before school starts? Any other suggestions that you have would be greatly appreciated.

Tim and Tyler wanted to know what to say in defense of Christianity when faced with a charge against it. Other people are interested in learning how to explain the Christian faith clearly to unbelievers. For example, Louis asked for help in sharing the gospel with a friend of his:

She was raised a Baptist and at one point in her life she became skeptical and suddenly none of the Christian claims made any sense to her. She claims she honestly wants to know, but has yet to hear a coherent answer to her inquiries. She is now a self-proclaimed agnostic. She's embraced pluralism; she feels there's a bit of truth in all religions and no one religion has the exclusive truth because God is too great for us to fully comprehend. When asked how she knows that Christianity isn't true, she says she doesn't, but the whole Jesus thing doesn't make any sense to her. Why did Jesus have to die? How does his death and resurrection "save" us? And why does she have to believe now, in this life? How does that make a difference? If God is a God of love, why not give us a chance to change our minds when we have proof He exists in the afterlife? I have a problem explaining this to her in very simple terminology so she can get it. Can you help?

Some inquiries speak to a more foundational need. A ministry leader came to my office the other day wondering why the old methods of evangelism weren't working for his congregation anymore. "What do we need to change?" he asked. He realized that there was something wrong at a fundamental level, but didn't know what it was.

This book will address all three types of questions, albeit in reverse order. Our focus will move from the broad and philosophical to the more precise and practical. This is necessary because the philosophical provides the foundation for the practical. If you are wrong or unsure about what you are trying to accomplish in a very general sense, you are much more likely to get sidetracked or bogged down in a conversation. So we will start the book by discussing the nature of religion and what that means in regard to the overarching goal of evangelism.

Then we will walk through the initial steps to take in framing a conversation properly. This is a key element to the book and provides an important distinguishing characteristic of my evangelistic model. As much as I appreciate all the apologetic and evangelistic resources available to us, most require immense amounts of memorization and expertise. Also, they leave the Christian on the defensive, always at the mercy of the next question or objection of the skeptic. My approach avoids those pitfalls. It offers a natural model for conversation that allows the believer to direct the discussion and can be implemented organically by almost anyone. Also, it is easily adaptable to various situations. Life doesn't always look like a university classroom and we aren't all trained professors; I try to take that into account in the pages that follow.

In part 2 we will elaborate on some of the most common misunderstandings skeptics have about God and discuss how to gently instruct them in the truth. Learning how to tell the story of the world in a winsome and easily understood way is essential to reaching unbelievers.

Finally, in part 3, we will talk about how to compare worldviews and address objections to Christianity. In doing so, we will learn a few arguments to present in support of the Christian worldview.

Before we begin, let's clarify what I mean by the word *skeptic*. Is this book only good for reaching hard-core atheists and agnostics? Not at all. I use the term in a very broad sense to refer to those who either aren't sure Christianity is true or are convinced that it isn't. That includes everyone from Richard Dawkins to the guy who has been going to your church for fifteen years but is starting to have some doubts about his faith. (It happens more than one might think.) Skeptics come in varying kinds and degrees, and the principles in this book can be applied across a wide spectrum of unbelief. Admittedly, the typical skeptic I had in mind while writing is what we might call a "secularist": an atheist or agnostic who has been soaking in the naturalistic ideas of the Western education and entertainment industry for too long and now has at least a vague sense that Christianity is not intellectually feasible. Most of the skeptics you run into will fall into this category, so that is where I focused. However, you can easily adapt this model to reach members of other religions and even spiritual seekers who are quite open to the faith but just have questions.

I've been talking to all kinds of skeptics for many years now, and I've made a ton of mistakes. I've tried to learn from those blunders, though, and over time I've realized that no matter who you are talking to, the key to a fruitful conversation is to frame the discussion properly and then direct it along a particular path. That is what we will learn in this book.

PART 1

A Framework for Fruitful Conversations

//////////// 1

No Selling Required

So you want to have that neighbor with the Darwin fish on her car over for coffee but you're worried about how the conversation might go. Perhaps you've got a business trip planned with that co-worker who has been reading *The God Delusion* on his lunch breaks and you are hoping to get a chance to discuss Jesus with him. Here is the first thing you should know: When it comes to talking about your religion, skeptics will usually expect you to try to sell them something.

That is not to say that your unbelieving neighbor and co-worker will be looking for church raffle tickets or Bibles for sale. I mean that they will assume that you will try to convince them to become Christians based on some benefit that Jesus offers. They will expect to hear about all of the good things that Christianity can do for them. They will view you, at least to some degree, as a snake-oil salesman or shady used-car guy. And even if you are not placed in quite so low a category, the bottom line is that when skeptics think of Christians doing evangelism, they envision hucksters plying their wares.

Unfortunately, they're not crazy for thinking this way. If your unbelieving acquaintances have spent any time at all around American religion over the past few decades, they probably have been treated as potential customers. The fact is that most churches sell a product, and most people expect them to do so.

Think about your community. If a spiritual seeker moved in and went to all the churches and religious gathering places in town in order to evaluate them and decide which one to join, what would he be told? Chances are he would hear about all the programs that each place offers and what personal needs would be met there. "Want some meaning in life? Inspiration? Peaceful meditation? Moral guidance? A great worship experience? Fun for you and the kids? Come to our church! Join our religion! We have all that and more! In fact, come this Sunday and you can even enjoy a free drink at our upscale coffee bar with this coupon!"

While they may not be aware of what they are doing, these churches are definitely selling a product and obviously believe that this is what people are looking for in a church.

They're probably right about that. According to a recent survey of over 35,000 people by the Pew Forum of Religion and Public Life, people are more willing than ever to change religions. It reported that "44% of adults have either switched religious affiliation, moved from being unaffiliated with any religion to being affiliated with a particular faith, or dropped any connection to a specific religious tradition altogether."[1] As columnist Timothy Shriver noted on the *Washington Post* website, religiously, we're doing what we do best: shopping. "And we're shopping for God." He goes on to say that "what's clear is that we're not going to accept religion based on the past. It's got to meet our spiritual needs or we'll move on."[2]

Exactly. Shriver did his own brief survey to find out what those needs are. He asked, "What's on your list when you go shopping for God?" Some people wanted joy, while others longed to be part of a humorous, compassionate, and loving community. One person wanted an "experience that helps me discover magic and peace and the spirit of the universe," while another noted that she is easily distracted and has a hard time focusing; she just wanted a place with some peace and quiet.[3] It seems like these folks are the type of people the churches mentioned above were catering to: "Whatever you want, we have it!"

By now you may be thinking, *What is wrong with shopping for God, or at least shopping for the good stuff associated with him? After all, following Jesus and being a part of the church does offer plenty of great benefits.* Indeed it does. However, to present those benefits as the first and primary reason to become a Christian or attend your church is to misunderstand the very nature of religion. More explicitly, to treat it as a consumer product is to fail to realize what religion actually is: a worldview. That is to say, religion is a set of beliefs that answers the big questions of life in regard to the nature of reality.

The term *religion* is notoriously hard to define. Every religion has different characteristics. However, for the sake of our conversation, let's point out something that is common to most: Religions are worldviews; they explain ultimate reality. Worldviews offer propositional truth claims about the most important questions of life. For example, "How did we get here?" "Why are we here?" "Is there a god?" "If so, what is he, she, or it like?" "What is wrong with the world?" "How can it be fixed?" "What happens when we die?" "How should we then live?"

The answers to these questions make up one's worldview. While not every worldview is considered a religion, I think a strong case can be made that almost all religions are worldviews. As such, they are not consumer products. Neither is true Christianity.

Let's spend some time expanding on these two contrasting views of religion in general and Christianity in particular.

Religion as a Consumer Product

On one hand, religion can be understood as a consumer product that meets your needs and desires. In this view, then, religion has value only inasmuch as it fulfills that role. As anyone who has ever operated a retail business knows, the value of a consumer product is whatever people will pay for it. Shoppers value things only according to how much they want or need them. Ultimately it doesn't matter how much the seller values a product, but how much the buyer values it. You may or may not think Starbucks coffee is worth five dollars a cup (or whatever it is going for these days), but evidently quite a few people do, so that is its current value.

On the other hand, let's say you open up a candy store specializing in spinach-flavored chocolate bars for five bucks apiece. Shockingly, nobody wants to buy them and you have to close up shop. You are convinced that each of your spinach bars is worth at least five dollars and probably more, but the potential customers won't give you five cents for them. Who is right about their value? The customer, of course. If people don't want to buy your product, they aren't wrong for rejecting it; they are the ones who determine its value. If customers decide they don't want or need something, there is no way to obligate or convince them to buy it.

If we apply this principle to religion, and see it as a consumer product, it doesn't matter how much the evangelist values his faith, but how much the seeker values it for himself. Therefore, people can pick and choose any religion they want (or a combination of religions), and nothing the preacher says is going to convince them they are wrong.

For example, let's say Jane Doe has a few needs and desires. She's lonely and a bit depressed; she has some guilt over her past actions; her kids could use some moral guidance, and she carries around a lot of stress from work. She realizes that religion is a good place to get these needs and desires met, so she considers her options. She has several open to her.

First, she might shop around until she finds one church that meets all those needs. An evangelical mega-church might fit the bill: Small groups to take care of her loneliness, a twelve-step program deals with her depression, a solid high school group teaches her kids, a sermon about God's forgiveness every Sunday morning handles the guilt, and a Saturday night meeting with a great band and Starbucks makes her utterly relaxed.

On the other hand, Jane might pick and choose from a variety of religions to meet her needs and desires. Just like we might go to Staples for paper and the grocery store for meat, Jane could treat her city as a religious smorgasbord in order to create just the right combination plate for her.

The Saturday night service and small groups might stay in the mix to take care of the loneliness, but for stress? The Hindu center down the street has yoga classes two times a week that seem to handle it just fine. As for the kids' moral guidance, the Muslim mosque is very strict, so that is a good place for them. What about the guilt? She can certainly find a secular psychologist who will tell her simply to deny it. The fact is, if religion is a consumer product, Jane can go to different places to get various needs met, all without thinking twice about it.

This type of scenario is not uncommon. Take Varun Gauri, for instance. As Stacy Weiner reports, for many years he was completely irreligious. However, now he has a daughter involved in many spiritual activities at a variety of local churches and schools. "Gauri says he wants to offer Yasmeen the moral foundation and spiritual guidance he believes religion can provide." Many other nonreligious parents are following suit. They don't practice any faith, but they "find themselves seeking the psychological, spiritual, and moral blessings they hope a religious background can bestow on their offspring."[4]

What they aren't seeking is the truth about reality. As a result they can hop from religion to religion, or claim several religions simultaneously without thinking twice about it. Consider Carol Christoffel of Zion, Illinois. According to Cathy Lynn Grossman in *USA Today*, Christoffel drifted through various Protestant denominations in her youth, dabbled in the Baha'i tradition for several years, and then was drawn into the healing practices of Native American spirituality. But she still calls herself a Christian.

> I'm a kind of bridge person between cultures. I agree with the teachings of Jesus and . . . I know many Christians like me who keep the Bible's social teachings and who care for the earth and for each other. I support people who do good wherever they are.[5]

Christoffel reminds me of Ann Holmes, the former Episcopal bishop from Seattle who claims to be both 100 percent Christian and 100 percent Muslim.[6] That kind of math is just fine for consumers of religion, as evidenced by the fact that Mr. Gauri and his wife are "dishing up a religious smorgasbord" for their kids:

> Islam from one grandma, Hindu from the other, a Quaker school, a Buddhist retreat and a bit of evangelical Christianity via their former nanny. As [Gauri's wife Ayesha] Khan acknowledges, "Only time will tell if we were creating great confusion or great enlightenment."[7]

Well, I have a guess on that. But these examples wouldn't bother our Jane Doe because she sees religion as an elixir, something that exists for her benefit. Particular religions have value and should be used, then, according to the extent that they are wanted or needed by Jane. She is the judge of religions, they do not judge her.

In this view, people use religion like they use hair spray: Whatever works for you is just fine and no one has any authority to tell you any different. After all, in sales, the customer is always right.

When talking to a skeptic, while you may not be tempted to use the selling points mentioned above, the fact is that you probably will want to offer some of your own: how Jesus changed your life, gave you hope for the future, forgave your sins. These are all good things that can be used later in the discussion. (We'll talk about them in chapters 11 and 12.) However, as a starting point, presenting these benefits as a reason to become a Christian may lead to this response: "While I am glad you found something that works for you, I have no need of God or religion—I am stronger and more courageous than to have to rely on ancient myths to get me through life." What are you going to say to that? If either of you is approaching religion as a consumer product, the skeptic has a perfectly valid point. If he doesn't want what you are offering, you don't have much recourse.

Religion as a Worldview

Now, if the skeptic you are talking to actually understands religion properly, presenting a list of selling points to him may lead to this response: "I don't really care what the benefits are. I don't think your religion is true, and therefore I am not going to believe it."

Sam Harris offers a good example of this in *Letter to a Christian Nation*. It seems he often gets told that he should become a Christian because Christianity produces moral people. In response he rightly asks, So what if it does? The real issue is whether or not it is true.

> Even if belief in God had a reliable, positive effect upon human behavior, this would not offer a reason to believe in God. One can believe in God only if one thinks that God actually exists. Even if atheism led straight to moral chaos, this would not suggest that the doctrine of Christianity is *true*. Islam might be true, in that case. Or all religions might function like placebos. As descriptions of the universe, they could be utterly false but, nevertheless, useful.[8]

This is exactly right. This is the proper view of religion. Religions, by their nature, do one thing without fail: explain ultimate reality. They are not like hair spray. They are like a road map. Like a map, they present what is supposed to be an accurate and objective account of certain aspects of our existence. They tell us what particular parts of the world are like. The most important question we must ask when considering a religion is not "What can it do for me?" or "Do I like it?" but "Is it true?" The one thing we need to know above all else is whether or not this religion accurately describes the nature of our existence. If it does not, it is ridiculous to join it, no matter what aspects of it we may find appealing. And if it does, it is ridiculous not to join it, no matter how many aspects of it we may find unappealing or how much it might help in providing a basis for morality.

C. S. Lewis spoke directly to this issue in an essay he was asked to write about whether or not one can lead a moral life without believing in Christianity. At the beginning of the piece, he wonders about the state of mind of those who made the request and worries that they are interested in Christianity not because they believe it to be true but that they find it helpful. Lewis derides "foolish preachers" who treat the faith as "a medicine" to help people. They need to realize, Lewis argues, that Christianity

> claims to give an account of *facts*—to tell you what the real universe is like. Its account of the universe may be true, or it may not. . . . If Christianity is untrue, then no honest man will want to believe it, however helpful it might be: if it is true, every honest man will want to believe it, even if it gives him no help at all.[9]

Dorothy Sayers seems to have Lewis's "foolish preachers" in mind in this passage about those who downplay and ignore Christian doctrine in an attempt to sell Christianity's consumer benefits:

> It is worse than useless for Christians to talk about the importance of Christian morality unless they are prepared to take their stand upon the fundamentals of Christian theology. It is a lie to say that dogma does not matter; it matters enormously. It is fatal to let people suppose that Christianity is only a mode of feeling; it is vitally necessary to insist that it is first and foremost a rational explanation of the universe. It is hopeless to offer Christianity as a vaguely idealistic aspiration of a simple and consoling kind; it is, on the contrary, a hard, tough, exacting, and complex doctrine, steeped in a drastic and uncompromising realism.[10]

Recently my family and I went on an epic road trip. We traveled through seven states and two provinces, putting over 4,400 miles on our minivan. Before we left I went down to the local office of the Automobile Club of Southern California to pick up some maps and brochures for our journey. I wanted to know what roads to take and what kinds of attractions we could expect to find along the way.

Imagine for a moment the following scenario: What if, when I arrived at the auto club, the cashier offered me a menu of maps from which to choose, each painting a radically different picture of what Western North America was like? One map portrayed that part of the continent as a swampy marshland with very few roads. Another showed it to be a flat prairie land, crisscrossed with roads every mile or two. A third map made North America out to be a small series of islands, navigable by car only on ferries. A fourth claimed that the geography varied wildly as one traveled inland from the ocean. It was drivable, but I would need to have a powerful vehicle to get across the myriad mountain ranges between me and my destination. Each map was written by a supposed authority in the field, each had its own adherents, and each was presented as an accurate description of the part of planet Earth on which I lived.

The purpose of this thought experiment is to show that this is what religions do; they claim to have accurate knowledge about where we live, where we are going, and what it will take to get there. They claim to know the truth about our existence.

At my imaginary auto club office, each map paints a radically different picture of the landscape and infrastructure on my route. How would I decide which one to use? I sure wouldn't ask, "Which map was printed using my favorite colors?" or "Which map gives me the shortest overall trip?" I also wouldn't respond, "Well, this one would allow me to mountain climb and ski, but this one would allow me to see crocodiles, and this one over here would be easier on gas, so that is a tough call. I guess I'll go with the mountains." Of course I wouldn't do that. The one question I would need to ask regarding the maps is "Which one is true?" It does not matter how much I may like the idea of having a nice view of the Everglades on my way to Seattle. If they aren't there, they aren't there, regardless of what the map tells me. If a map is false, there is no point in following it, no matter how many aspects of it may "work best for me." And if the map is true, I must follow it, no matter how much I may dislike certain aspects of the reality it describes.

This is true of religion as well. It is absolutely silly to accept or reject a religion based on something you happen to like or dislike about it. "Well, I just don't want there to be a hell, so I have to reject Christianity." That is simply nonsensical. If hell exists, it exists, regardless of your opinions. The bottom line is that we must pick a religion (a worldview) based on whether or not we think it is true.

Religion is not a product, so parishioners should not be consumers and evangelists should not be salespeople. To misunderstand this is incredibly dangerous, because the stakes are so high. Imagine if I tried to reach a vacation spot that doesn't even exist using a map that is completely false. It would be very frustrating, and I would waste a lot of time, effort, and money. That is why we plan our trips carefully and use only trustworthy guides. How much more then, should we search for a trustworthy guide to the journey of life. The destiny of our souls is on the line. It is one thing to be wrong about whether or not a great fishing lake exists and how to get there. It is quite another to be wrong about whether or not heaven exists and how to get *there*.

Are there temporal benefits to religion? Of course. But those benefits cannot be reasons to choose a religion. Should the church be serving others and meeting people's temporal needs? Absolutely. However, this service must be accompanied by evangelism. It is not itself evangelism. Evangelism is proclaiming the message of the gospel and trying to convince people it is true, because we understand that if a worldview is false, it must be rejected, and if it is true, it must be accepted.

Jesus ran into the consumerist mind-set during his ministry. After he provided food for the people, a large crowd started following him hoping to get more free stuff. Jesus scolded them because they had the wrong mentality. They should have recognized the miraculous provision of food not only as an act of love but as evidence supporting his claim to be the Son of God. They were chasing after food that spoils rather than the bread of life (John 6:26–27). They were in the presence of truth himself, but because they were seeking to fulfill their temporal needs and desires rather than find truth, they missed it.

The only reason to become a Christian is because Christianity is true, and the only reason to reject another worldview is because it is false. This is the mind-set with which you should approach a skeptic. You don't want to frame the conversation as a sales pitch, but as a pursuit of truth. You are not there to debate the good effects of religion versus the bad effects of skepticism. Rather, you want to discuss which worldview is more likely to be true. In the next chapter we will expand on how to have this type of conversation.

////////////// **2**

The Big Picture

Establishing the Topic of Conversation

I often get calls from atheists and other skeptics wanting to debate me over some particular objection they have to Christianity. For example, a listener named Justin wondered why God didn't do more to abolish slavery in Old Testament times. A different caller named Jason explained that he rejected the Christian faith, after twenty-five years of being a believer, because he thought the idea of hell was cruel and unjust. Other listeners have wanted to dispute whether the resurrection of Christ actually happened or argue about how it is possible that Jesus was born of a virgin or how we can have free will in heaven. The list of objections is endless.

The natural response to these charges is to try to answer them immediately. However, that is exactly what we must not do. In this chapter I will explain why we should direct the topic to a discussion of worldviews instead.

When a caller presents an objection to Christianity, my response is always the same: I tell her that I would be glad to talk about her topic. Indeed, we will examine some of the specific objections mentioned above later in this book. However, I insist that her specific issue cannot be the first thing we talk about. Nor can it be the only thing. Rather, we need to discuss whatever particular objection she has within the context of discussing worldviews in general. That is to say, before we can talk about slavery in the Old Testament or whether Jesus walked on water, we need to talk about what kind of universe we live in. We need to try to establish what is most likely to be true in regard to the big questions of life we discussed in the last chapter. How did we get here? Why are we here? What happens when we die? Is reality supernatural or is matter all there is? How should we then live?

The key here is to stay very "big picture." You don't want to get goaded into a fight over the first objection presented. Rather, you want to discuss grand narratives. You want to talk about which story of the universe is more reasonable to believe: Christianity, or something else? In other words, you want to set up a broad comparison of worldviews.

Your overall argument is going to be that Christianity is the worldview that best accounts for the evidence. Compared to any other worldview an unbeliever cares to offer, Christianity most adequately and comprehensively makes sense of life as we experience it every day, answering the big questions of life in a way that doesn't disregard any facet of our lives. Because of this, it is most likely to be true.

This is called "worldview hypothesis" evangelism. I will expand on how to use it throughout the book. For now I simply want to emphasize that it is very important to establish the proper topic for conversation at the very beginning of your interaction. Rather than get sidetracked into an argument over a specific objection, you need to establish that worldview comparison is the topic right up front and then be strong enough to stick with it. This may involve making a simple statement like this: "I am more than happy to discuss your objection in the proper context, but before we can do that we need to establish that context by talking about worldviews. I am convinced that Christianity best accounts for the evidence and is the most reasonable worldview to accept—it is most likely to be true."

Again, I will teach the specifics of this argument and how to winsomely present it later on. For now, let's look at a few reasons why it is so important that you establish worldviews as the topic of discussion at the beginning of your talk rather than get bogged down trying to answer one or two objections to Christianity.

Biblical Faith Is Not Irrational

The first reason to establish worldviews as the topic is to highlight from the start that you welcome rationality and an examination of the evidence. In comparing worldviews, your goal will be to figure out which theory of reality best explains the facts. By emphasizing this up front you are making clear that your position relies on reason and data. You are saying, "I am interested in putting worldviews under examination and I just want to establish the proper framework. I trust that we each are seeking truth and are willing to examine the evidence to find it."

This approach will probably surprise the skeptics you talk to. Most consider themselves to be harbingers of reason, as opposed to Christians who take blind leaps of irrational faith. They assume that the evidence is on their side and that Christians either don't care about evidence or don't want to look at it. For example, when I spoke to Edwin Kagin of American Atheists on my radio show,[1] he suggested that believing in the God of the Bible was the same as accepting the existence of invisible unicorns, obviously implying that there is no evidence for such a claim and Christians who believe it do so in spite of that fact and with an abject refusal to think through the silliness of their position. This is why Daniel Dennett has encouraged skeptics to call themselves "brights"[2] in order to distinguish themselves from dim-witted believers who have to put their brains in their back pockets in order to believe. These skeptics think that to have "faith" is to accept something as true even though you have no reason to! As Richard Dawkins puts it, faith is "blind trust, in the absence of evidence, even in the teeth of evidence."[3] It is "an evil precisely because it requires no justification and brooks no argument."[4]

This is ridiculous. While Dawkins may have a point in regard to how other religions define faith, this is certainly not the Christian definition of the term. Unfortunately, many Christians perpetuate this fallacy because they don't realize that God wants them to be thinking people who follow the evidence where it leads. Because the idea that Christianity is fideistic is so widespread, I want to take some time to examine just how opposite it is to true biblical religion.

The fact is that Christianity welcomes an examination of the evidence. Indeed, it relies on it! As we examine the definition of faith found in the Bible, we will see that faith in God is directly tied to thinking properly about the evidence he has provided us.

According to the author of the book of Hebrews, "Faith is confidence in what we hope for and assurance about what we do not see" (Hebrews 11:1). Now, some might look at that and say, "There you go. It's right there. To have faith is to believe in something you can't see. In other words, you don't have any evidence for it!" Not at all. Faith in this passage, and in the rest of the Bible, primarily deals with the future. It is to trust that God is good and that he will do what he has promised he will do. We do not see what we are hoping for because it hasn't happened yet. However, this is not to say that we do not have any evidence on which to base our trust. Quite the contrary: Biblical faith is always based on evidence. Those people in the Bible who have faith trust that God will do what they hope for *because they have seen evidence that he is trustworthy*! For example, what gave David the faith to face Goliath? The fact that he had already experienced God's protection and victory in facing a lion and a bear! David had good evidence of God's power; therefore, he was able to have faith (1 Samuel 17:34–37).

This is God's pattern throughout history. He doesn't ask his followers to believe without any evidence or in spite of the evidence. Rather, God gives people evidence and then asks them to trust him in light of it. Faith is to be based on evidence; it is not something that is to develop without evidence. Here are a couple of quick examples, one from each of the Testaments.

When Moses appeared before Pharaoh to demand the release of the slaves, he explained that he was there on behalf of the Lord, the God of Israel. Pharaoh refused his request with a question: "Who is the LORD, that I should obey him and let Israel go?" (Exodus 5:2). There were plenty of gods in Egypt, and Pharaoh didn't think this one was worth worrying about. Notice that God did not respond with an appeal to "just believe." He didn't ask Pharaoh to obey despite the lack of evidence. Instead, just as God gave Moses several signs of his power when Moses was hesitant to obey (Exodus 4:1–14), he proceeded to give Pharaoh and the people of Egypt a series of signs as evidence that they should trust and obey as well.

By the end of the plagues, the answer to the question "Who is the Lord?" would be made clear through a display of God's power, not a feeble request for blind acceptance of a proposition. God then took his people through the Red Sea (Exodus 14), miraculously provided them with food and water (Exodus 15:22–17:7), and supernaturally defeated their enemies in battle (Exodus 17:8–16). All of these actions were intended to give evidence to the people that God was worthy of their trust. They were to have faith that God would get them to the Promised Land because they had good evidence that he was willing and able to do just that. When the people got to the edge of the Promised Land and then refused to enter it out of fear, God became angry precisely because they did not take into account all the evidence he had already presented to them (Numbers 14:10–12).

God's revelation of himself in Jesus followed the same pattern as his revelation of himself to Pharaoh and the Israelites. Jesus presented evidence to back up his claim that he was the God who had power and authority over all. Just as the plagues showed God's power over every realm of existence (the gods of Egypt and the natural forces of Earth), Jesus' miracles showed his power and authority over the very same entities.

The famous story of Jesus calming the sea is illustrative.

> A furious squall came up, and the waves broke over the boat, so that it was nearly swamped. Jesus was in the stern, sleeping on a cushion. The disciples woke him and said to him, "Teacher, don't you care if we drown?"
>
> He got up, rebuked the wind and said to the waves, "Quiet! Be still!" Then the wind died down and it was completely calm.
>
> He said to his disciples, "Why are you so afraid? Do you still have no faith?"
>
> Mark 4:37–40

Notice the word *still* in Jesus' last sentence. The key to understanding his rebuke of the disciples is to realize that they had already seen Jesus do many miraculous signs and wonders. He had shown his power and goodness in casting out demons and healing many sick and lame (Mark 1:21–3:12). The proper response to the storm would have been to remember that Jesus had been willing and able to exert authority over every other realm of existence and surmise that he could handle this too. Jesus was not asking them to trust him to keep them safe on the boat for no good reason. He had already given them evidence. *Based on the evidence*, they were to have faith. We are to have faith for the very same reason.

A Cumulative Case

Our belief that Christianity is true is not based on just one piece of data. This is a second reason for not getting sidetracked into a debate about a specific objection. To only talk about one specific issue may give the impression that it is the only one you have or that the case for Christianity will rise or fall based on how you are able to answer one question or difficulty. While some issues, such as the resurrection of Christ, do necessarily need to be defended and answered, the Christian faith does not rely on a single argument or solitary bit of evidence. Rather, we can build certitude that Christianity is true based on a cumulative case. There is a convergence of evidences that support the faith and, whether or not we are able to support each piece of evidence in the same manner and with the same degree of certainty, the cumulative case is very strong. For example, even if we don't have a solid, concise answer for an alleged biblical contradiction, we can still remain confident in the truth of Christianity based on the large amount of evidence we have from such a broad range of sources.

We base our knowledge of everyday facts on a cumulative case all the time. Thomas Dubay provides an example:

> I know that Istanbul is a city in Turkey, even though I have never been there and the concept has no necessary inner light to it. I am sure of this city's existence because of a convergence of independent evidences. I have seen it indicated in geography books and on road maps. I have noted it perhaps in airline timetables and travel advertising. I may have a friend who lives in Istanbul and sends me letters with the city postmark upon them, and my letters in return reach their destination when so marked. I have heard television news broadcasts and read newspaper and magazine articles dealing with the city. There is no possible explanation for this agreement of independent evidences but the sheer fact that the city does exist. Even though I cannot prove each bit of evidence, all these independent and unrelated reasons taken together so reinforce one another that the conclusion could not be mistaken. Doubt is baseless and foolish. My mind has the ability to grasp the whole of the situation and to perceive the necessity to which the agreements point.[5]

So let's say an "Istanbul skeptic" wanted to debate me about the existence of that city. He could focus on one particular piece of evidence and try to debunk it. For example, perhaps he found an error in a world atlas that caused him to doubt the veracity of that particular atlas. "You can't really trust these reference books," he might say, "therefore it is unreasonable to believe that Istanbul exists." I could attempt to defeat his argument by defending the reliability of atlases, but it would be better for me to start the conversation by emphasizing that world atlases are not the only reason I believe Istanbul exists. It's not that I won't address the issue of whether geographical reference books are trustworthy, it's that I don't want to start by getting bogged down with a piece of data that is only one small part of the evidence that I have. To focus all of our time on atlases would not do justice to the subject of whether or not Istanbul exists.

Now, I don't happen to know anyone who actually disbelieves in the existence of Istanbul, so let's move on to a more realistic example. On July 20, 1969, astronauts Neil Armstrong and Buzz Aldrin stepped out of their spacecraft and walked on the moon. At least that is what I believe happened. Not everyone does. Some people think the Apollo 11 mission was a hoax perpetrated on a gullible public by NASA. They believe the "moon landing" actually took place on a sound stage firmly planted on terra firma.

For evidence to support this notion, conspiracy theorists point to the official pictures of the event. They argue that some of the images contain shadows that are at the wrong angle and that the footage is filled with other oddities that would be inconsistent with a real moon landing. I think each of the objections can be addressed and debunked. However, before doing that I would point out to someone who denies the moon landing that pictures are not the only data that support a moon landing and that my case does not rest on whether or not I can explain the angle of a shadow on one or two photographs.

Applying this principle to a discussion of Christianity, the skeptic may want to focus on inconsistencies in the Bible or offer an alternative theory as to why people believe in the resurrection. That is fine, and those issues can and must be addressed in due time. However, it is better to establish at the beginning of the conversation the broad scope of your argument. Before discussing any one particular piece of data or a specific objection to Christianity, I like to quickly list about a dozen pieces of data that I think support Christianity. (We will discuss these data points and how to use them in chapter 9.) The reason I do this is simply to stake my claim to a comprehensive case for Christianity. By offering this list, I am not claiming that I need to debate each point with the other person. Frankly, we may not get to any of them. I am simply assuring that I won't get into a situation in which I am putting unnecessary emphasis on one point.

The Skeptic Needs More

Another reason not to get sucked into immediately addressing an objection to Christianity is that the skeptic needs much more than this. That is not to say that he doesn't need his objection answered. It is simply to point out that trying to answer the objection or question quickly may actually be detrimental. When I received the email from Louis, mentioned earlier, about what he should say to his friend who had lost her faith, I started to write a quick response. Then I realized that there simply was no quick response I could give. The girl in question needed more than just a question or two answered. She needed an entirely new approach to religion and a long course in history and Christian doctrine, among many other things. I found myself wanting to download my decades of study and experience into Louis so that he could then do the same to his friend. However, reality doesn't work that way. There is no quick fix for the situation she was in and it is often pointless to try to offer one. It is much wiser to try to step back a bit and broaden the topic to a foundational level. Start talking worldviews and the nature of religion, and then go from there. It will take some time, but it will be worth it in the end.

Keeping the Discussion Focused

A fourth reason to avoid jumping in with both feet in response to a specific objection is that even if you have a quick answer to whatever the unbeliever presents, they usually will ignore that answer and simply throw something else at you, often without ever admitting that the first objection was even addressed. For example, the skeptic might open the conversation by flatly stating that there is no evidence for the resurrection of Christ. In response, you start to present some. Before you can get two sentences into your defense of the historicity of the resurrection, you are likely going to be hearing about all the historical atrocities supposedly committed in Jesus' name.

There is no reason to allow this to happen. One of the easiest ways to avoid it is to establish right up front that you are more than happy to talk about any specific objections the skeptic has in due time and in the proper context, but that context must be established first. Before you can talk about specific issues, you need to talk about worldviews. By focusing the discussion on the broad topic of worldview comparison, hopefully you can keep the skeptic from veering too far afield.

Dealing With the Burden of Proof Issue

A final reason to establish worldviews as the topic is to ensure that the burden of proof is placed on both sides of the debate. Greg Koukl offers this good advice:

> Christians should not be the only ones who have to defend their views. Reject the impulse to counter every assertion someone manufactures. Don't try to refute every tale spun out of thin air. Instead, steer the burden of proof back on the other person's shoulders. Make them give you *reasons*, not just a point of view. It's not your job to defeat their claim. It's their job to defend it.[6]

One good way to make sure the skeptic is forced to defend his views is to make the conversation about worldviews rather than just his objections to Christianity. As we will see, a major component of the worldview discussion model that I will teach you is to find out what the skeptic believes and what evidence he has to support those assertions. If you spend your time only focused on addressing his objections to Christianity, the burden of proof will unnecessarily stay on your shoulders.

Skeptics are often very reluctant to allow the conversation to be about anything but attacking Christianity and often flatly refuse to explain their worldview or admit that they even have one. One reason for this is that many skeptics are simply anti-Christian and haven't actually thought about the subject much beyond that. They reject Christianity, but they do not favor much of anything. In other words, they don't accept a Christian worldview, but most of them have not thought through whether or not there is a more reasonable alternative. Do we all live in someone's dream? Are there many gods? Do we live in a closed system of cause and effect in which matter is all there is? If Christianity isn't true, what is the most likely explanation for the nature of reality? Most skeptics don't think along these lines.[7] By helping your conversation partner to do so you will force her to start evaluating whether or not she actually has a rational system of belief of her own rather than just a few objections to someone else's.

Which Worldview Is the "Fringe" Theory?

As you probably surmised by now, I think skeptics have much more in common with those who deny a moon landing than Christians do. Although skeptics like to present themselves as the ones who follow the evidence and think clearly about these issues, if you follow the model presented in this book, more often than not you will find that this simply isn't the case. Christianity is the worldview to which the evidence points. Those who deny this are often motivated not by an honest pursuit of truth, but rather a desire to avoid the implications of Christianity being true. The first step in making this clear is to establish the topic as a comparison of worldviews rather than a particular objection to Christianity.

The State of
the Doubter's Knowledge

Be Slow to Speak and Quick to Listen

The email from Bill started out with what seemed to me to be some thinly veiled mockery: "I was a Christian until my mid-twenties, when, for the first time in my life, I started actually using my head and realized that it was all baloney." Perhaps I was tired and irritable that day, and maybe I read too much into the email, but my first response was to start typing up a quick reply that went something like this: "Really? Really!? You finally started thinking and of course that led you to abandon Christianity? So I guess everyone who has ever actually 'used their head' has come to the same conclusion as you and become an atheist? I suppose that every Christian in the history of the world who hasn't abandoned their faith has been an unthinking idiot? Is that it? Augustine, Aquinas, Lewis: All numskulls? Is that what you are saying? Give me a break."

Let me assure you that this is not the way to react to an opening salvo from a skeptic. I explained in the last chapter that we need to be very careful about not starting a conversation by defending a particular objection to Christianity. In this chapter I am going to expand on that notion a bit by arguing that we should not start a conversation by defending Christianity at all, especially with the attitude that I displayed. Rather, we should humbly and gently listen and ask questions in an attempt to learn as much as we can about what the skeptic believes and where he is coming from.

The thesis of this chapter is that the first step to having a fruitful worldview discussion is to find out what the skeptic believes. Specifically, you want to find out first what is his own worldview, and second, what he understands to be the Christian worldview. In other words, you want to know how he answers those questions we talked about in chapter 1 and how he thinks Christianity answers them.

For example, I should have written something like this to Bill: "That's very interesting. I'd love to hear about your intellectual journey. Could you tell me a bit about that?" I could then have followed up with, "I'm particularly interested in what you found to be a more reasonable worldview than Christianity. I understand that you don't think Christianity correctly answers the big questions of life, but what answers *did* you conclude were right? What do you think *is* true about the world? Where do you think we came from? According to your worldview, what is the purpose of life and how should we then live? And what happens after we die?" Then, after interacting about that for a while, I would keep the questions coming, but switch to inquiries about the skeptic's view of Christianity. For example: "You told me that you used to be a Christian but now have rejected Christianity. Could you tell me about the Christianity you abandoned? According to your understanding, how does the Christian worldview answer the big questions of life? What is the story of the world according to the Bible as you read it?"

One of the keys to this stage is not to do a lot of talking. There is no need to preach or present an argument or even rebut what the skeptic is saying. Your goal here is simply to ask questions, listen, and learn. You will have your chance to talk later on. At the beginning, the focus should be on allowing the unbeliever to share. This is very important for several reasons.

Build Relationship, Not Animosity

First, the act of sincerely asking questions, in and of itself, generally defuses any animosity that might be present and avoids creating any new ill feelings. As Hugh Hewitt writes, "When you ask a question, you are displaying interest in the person asked. . . . Most people are not queried on many, if any, subjects. Their opinions are not solicited. To ask them is to be remembered fondly as a very interesting and gracious person in your own right."[1] Greg Koukl adds "[Questions] invite genial interaction on something the other person cares a lot about: her own ideas."[2]

Getting into a heated argument is not going to do anyone any good. In fact, it will usually just turn the skeptic against Christianity even more than she already is. Jumping into an emotionally charged adversarial discussion will only make things worse. On the other hand, showing interest in the other person by asking questions will generally calm any passions that might be aroused and open up a door for a fruitful conversation. As Proverbs tells us, "A gentle answer turns away wrath, but a harsh word stirs up anger" (15:1). This is one reason Paul tells Timothy: "Don't have anything to do with foolish and stupid arguments, because you know they produce quarrels. And the Lord's servant must not be quarrelsome but must be kind to everyone . . ." (2 Timothy 2:23–24). Randy Newman points out, "Many an evangelizing Christian has won the battle but lost the war by not avoiding an ugly argument."[3] Asking questions is a great response to an initial outburst by a skeptic in that it shows you genuinely care about the other person and are willing to let her have the first say. This will go a long way toward making your conversation pleasant and productive.

Listen and Learn

A second reason not to go into a conversation with guns blazing is that it is often counterproductive; you end up shooting at and destroying the wrong target. In other words, Christians who start a conversation by doing a lot of talking often address a person who does not exist and a position he does not hold. If we start preaching and making arguments before learning what the other person is all about, there is very little chance that we will address the proper concerns. It is ridiculous to assume that just because a person self-identifies with a label such as *atheist* or *agnostic* that we know what he actually believes or what his attitude will be toward us. The better tactic is to ask questions first in order to learn who and what we are actually dealing with.

In regard to the other person's attitude, we must avoid being cynical about his motives or heart condition and give him the benefit of the doubt. If my experience with Bill (and far too many others, unfortunately, especially early in my ministry) is any indication, it is very easy to enter a conversation with a cynical perspective of the other person's attitude and motives: "He probably thinks I am a jerk for being a Christian, and therefore he is obviously a jerk, so I'm going to go into this thing armed for battle. At the first sign of sarcasm or condescension, I'm going to let him have a double-barrel dose of his own medicine!" This is simply anti-Christian and actually a sin. We are to love our enemies (Matthew 5:44) and consider others higher than ourselves (Philippians 2:3). Attacking them violates both of these commands and will not advance the kingdom.

If I had asked questions instead of jumping all over Bill, I would have learned (as I did later in our interaction) that he was actually a decent guy who had some legitimate concerns with Christianity as he understood it. In this he was like many atheists who reject the faith not because of their personal hatred of Christians or of Jesus, but because they have a view of Christianity that deserves to be rejected. C. S. Lewis wrote that "Very little of the opposition we meet is inspired by malice or suspicion. It is based on genuine doubt, and often on doubt that is reasonable in the state of the doubter's knowledge."[4] Lewis realized that personal issues are often not the things keeping people from Jesus. The real problem is ignorance. Unbelievers have false notions of what Christianity teaches and don't realize how much strong evidence there is to support orthodox doctrines. We will talk about some of those false notions in part 2, but for now I want to emphasize that you will never get to the point of being able to address them if you don't start by asking questions.

Questioning also helps to clarify those beliefs. Too many religious conversations involve people talking past each other because they haven't taken the time to find out what the other person actually believes. The result is that each side tries to knock down a straw-man version of the other's position. The skeptic argues against a version of Christianity that the believer does not hold, and the Christian attacks an atheistic worldview that the unbeliever does not hold. Then they wonder why the conversation never gets anywhere.

For example, I once debated Dr. Robert Price about the historicity of Jesus' resurrection. Even though I went first in the debate, in his opening statement Dr. Price debunked a series of arguments I had not presented and exposed the foolishness of a bunch of doctrines that I did not even accept. In my response, I mentioned that I was not sure whom Dr. Price was debating during his presentation, but it didn't seem to be me. He was rejecting a Christianity that I reject as well.

In *Christian Apologetics*, Douglas Groothuis devotes a chapter to "Distortions of the Christian Worldview—Or the God I Don't Believe In." He notes that Christianity is falsely accused of being racist, sexist, anti-intellectual, and imperialistic, among many other defects. Unfortunately, "due to their popularity and the passion with which they are promoted, distorted accounts of Christianity keep many from pondering the genuine Christian message."[5] When people hear you are a Christian they will often have a picture of Christianity in their minds that you wouldn't come close to recognizing. You want to make sure that you are not defending a god that you don't believe in, and the first step in doing this is to find out what the other person thinks about God.

You also want to make sure you are not attacking a worldview that they don't believe in. In the same way that atheists usually will have a distorted view of what you believe, you will have a distorted view of what they believe. To start debating the two positions without clarifying what it is that each person actually means by *Christian* and *atheist* (or *agnostic* or *skeptic* or whatever) is the height of folly and will only lead to frustration. Therefore, the first step must be to ask questions and learn what it is the unbeliever actually believes.

PART 2

What Skeptics Need to Know About God

////////////// **4**

Love and the Meaning of Life

Christianity According to a Typical Skeptic

"An Atheist Meets God" is a five-minute animated YouTube video that has been watched two and a half million times. In it, an atheist is run over by a bus and finds himself at the entrance to heaven, face-to-face with God. In the subsequent exchange, a petty, unjust, and angry deity explains why the skeptic will soon be thrown into hell: Even though the unbeliever was in fact a good person, because he did not praise and worship God and believe everything written in the Bible, he will be punished with eternal torment.[1]

In the previous chapter we learned how important it is to understand what the skeptic believes Christianity teaches. You want to know how she thinks the church and the Bible answer those big questions of life. In other words, you want to learn the Christian story according to the skeptic. "An Atheist Meets God" is a good example of what you will hear. Almost inevitably, this process reveals that the skeptic has a very ill-informed view of God's purposes in creating and redeeming humankind. Indeed, her understanding of the Christian worldview will usually sound something like this (or at least pick up on some of the plot points mentioned here):

God seems to be some sort of egomaniac who created people to tell him how great he is. He apparently has some sort of inferiority complex or lack within himself that needs to be filled by people's worship.

He also likes giving people silly and arbitrary rules and then punishing them unjustly for not keeping them. In fact, he even punishes people for the sins of others! For example, for some strange reason we are held responsible for Adam and Eve breaking that crazy rule about not eating apples.

After Adam and Eve fell, God made even more silly and arbitrary rules and rituals for people on earth to follow, threatening them with eternal torture if they couldn't keep them, even though it seems there is really no way to keep them all. Also, these rules seem to change over time or be selectively applied to different people at different times or something—the whole rules thing is very confusing and contradictory.

The same goes for the nation of Israel. Apparently God chose a group of people to go wipe out other groups of people?

As for how to avoid hell, it does seem God is willing to let some people off the hook. Those who intellectually assent to the proposition that he exists or acknowledge that Jesus was God or repent or some such thing get forgiven of their so-called sins and get a pass into heaven.

God doesn't give us any evidence supporting any of these claims other than to drop a book out of the sky that we have to accept on "faith." In other words, we have to deny science and reason and every other means of gathering knowledge and just accept that the Bible is true, even though it is self-contradictory and teaches things that science has proven to be false (such as the age of the earth, etc.).

Those who somehow hear this message and believe (and most people in history haven't heard it) will get to spend forever holding hands and singing low-quality praise choruses to God (eternal boredom is the prize) while those that never heard and all atheists will spend forever getting tortured.

To sum up this view, God is "cruel, vindictive, capricious and unjust."[2] As Richard Dawkins writes,

The God of the Old Testament is arguably the most unpleasant character in all fiction: jealous and proud of it; a petty, unjust, unforgiving control-freak; a vindictive, bloodthirsty ethnic cleanser; a misogynistic, homophobic, racist, infanticidal, genocidal, filicidal, pestilential, megalomaniacal, sadomasochistic, capriciously malevolent bully.[3]

As many have pointed out,[4] this view shows a shocking ignorance of the theological reflection that has taken place over the past four thousand years. In Terry Eagleton's review of Dawkins' *The God Delusion* he writes, "Imagine someone holding forth on biology whose only knowledge of the subject is the *Book of British Birds*, and you have a rough idea of what it feels like to read Richard Dawkins on theology."[5] Or to use Rodney Stark's words: "To expect to learn anything about important theological problems from Richard Dawkins or Daniel Dennett is like expecting to learn about medieval history from someone who had only read *Robin Hood*."[6] One more, from Edward Feser: "One gets the impression that the bulk of their education in Christian theology consisted of reading *Elmer Gantry* while in college, supplementing that with a viewing of *Inherit the Wind* and a Sunday morning spent channel-surfing televangelists."[7]

We won't address all of Dawkins' specific charges here (Paul Copan's *Is God a Moral Monster?* is a great resource in this area), but in this section of the book I do want to examine some of the more fundamental flaws in the typical skeptic's version of the story of the world according to Christianity.

Before I do, however, let's note that skeptics are not the only ones with terrible theology. Many Christians don't properly understand the faith either. Indeed, many of the doctrinal positions Dawkins tries to knock down have been set up by believers, as he notes in the preface to the paperback version of *The God Delusion*. He rightly points out that he is not setting up a straw-man argument against Christianity so much as he is simply addressing the beliefs of one very popular subset of Christianity, one which he labels fundamentalism.[8] Fair enough. However, all that means is that one subset of Christianity is just as wrong as Dawkins in their understanding of God. They both need to be educated in the truth of the historic orthodox faith.

For example, you may have noticed that capriciousness is a strong theme that runs throughout the skeptics' story. They see God as arbitrary and unfair; he does stuff for no other reason than he decided to do it. In other words, God's story could have been fundamentally different. He could have defined sin differently, for instance, or found some other way than Jesus' death and resurrection to deal with our disobedience to his random rules. Because of this, thinks the skeptic, it is pointless to try and make too much sense of God's actions or to expect them to be consistently just. There is no essential rhyme or reason to the story of the Bible. God does what he does and we just have to deal with that. This notion is false, as we will see in the following chapters, but one can understand how the skeptic came up with it. After all, it is widely believed within many Christian circles.

For instance, I recently read a skit in a children's curriculum book about the work of Christ on the cross. The instructions went something like this: First, choose a kid from the audience that you are sure does not know that much about Christian theology. Have him come to the front of the group and explain that he has been selected to take part in a test. He will be asked a question and if he answers correctly he will receive a bowl of candy (or some other prize of your choosing). However, if he gets the question wrong, he will get a pie in the face. You then ask the child to define substitutionary atonement. When he is unable to answer, start preparing the whipped cream in a plate for the big event. However, just before you hit him with it, a person from the audience (someone you have prearranged) should jump up and run forward, offering to take the child's punishment on herself. You then smash the pie into the substitute's face, explaining that, in the same way, Jesus was our substitute. He took our penalty on the cross.

Now, I suppose I can see some small glimmer of truth in this skit, but it is overshadowed by the fact that the instructor—the God figure—comes across as capricious and unfair. Think about what the child at the front would be thinking. If he is anything like me, it would be this: *What did I do to deserve to be sitting here? How am I supposed to know what substitutionary atonement means? What does that have to do with anything anyway? Why should I get a pie in the face for not being able to answer correctly? And what sense does it make for someone else to take a pie that neither of us deserves? The whole thing is silly and pointless.*

The kid would be right. The whole thing is silly and pointless because it is completely arbitrary and unjust. The test was made up by the instructor and impossible to pass, the punishment bore no relationship to the "offense," and the solution to the made-up "problem" was similarly random. The whole situation was contrived. The skit writer made the instructor seem capricious.

God is not like that. We will discuss the redemptive work of Jesus in more detail later in the book, but for now I just want to emphasize the fact that God's actions are not arbitrary, unjust, or completely beyond our understanding. There is a unity of purpose to the story of Scripture that reveals a loving father graciously and consistently working to draw people into the relationship for which they were created. As we walk through some of the most commonly misunderstood aspects of that mission, we will see that God has good reasons for all that he does.

Worship and Sacrifice

In this chapter we will address God's desire for worship and sacrifice. As seen in the "An Atheist Meets God" video, skeptics see this as evidence that God is motivated by lack and cruelty. They look at God as a schoolyard bully who makes little kids give him their lunch money in order to feel better about himself. In this view, God needs people to keep telling him how great he is because he has some sort of inferiority complex.

The answer to this charge is that God is not motivated by lack or cruelty but by an overflow of love. God doesn't need anything. Quite the contrary; God has so much of one thing in particular that it naturally runs over: love. Love, not cruelty, is the reason that God desires worship and sacrifice from his creatures. To support and explain this assertion, let's start by defining love.

The Nature of Love

Love is first and foremost a response to value. It is a recognition and affirmation that someone is objectively valuable. To love is to proclaim to the beloved that he or she is of great worth. Many of us have experienced this, of course, in the very first stages of a relationship: You see that girl or boy across the room and think, *Wow! I've found someone very special!* Exactly. You don't love someone you think is worthless. Love is not present or possible if one does not think the other person has any value.

Second, love is the giving of oneself sacrificially for the good of another. To love someone is not just to say that he or she is valuable, but it is to act sacrificially for that person's good. It's not enough to think that a person is great, or even to tell them that several times a day; we must act in a way that benefits that person. We don't just love in word and thought, but in our actions (1 John 3:18).

Third, love is the desire for unity with another person. You want to be together, but even more than that you want to be one with that person, at least to some degree. (Romantic love has a higher degree of union than friendship, for example, but each involves a degree of union.) To love someone is to hurt when they hurt and rejoice when they rejoice. It is to know them as they know themselves. This union is only possible as people share time and experiences together. This longing for union includes a longing to simply be with the beloved. Parents who say they love their kids but never want to spend time with them do not actually love those children according to this definition.

Much more could be said about the nature of love, but let's leave it at that for now and talk about where I got this definition of love. Is it arbitrary? Did I just make it up out of thin air? No. It is based on the nature of God, who is love.

By that I mean that God has eternally existed in a mutually self-giving relationship within the Trinity. The Trinity involves the three persons of the Godhead recognizing the infinite value of each other and giving sacrificially of themselves to each other. Love, as I described it, is the essence of God's existence.

This means that love is the most basic thing in all of reality. As Jean Daniélou writes, "Without doubt the master key to Christian theology . . . is contained in the statement that the

Trinity of Persons constitutes the structure of Being, and that love is therefore as primary as existence."[9] In other words, love is foundational to everything; love is what reality is all about.

As such, love is the reason God created the universe and everything in it. Creation is not an arbitrary act of a capricious God. Rather, it is the necessary result of a loving God. Creation is the natural consequence of love. New life and a larger family, which is what God created when he made Adam and Eve, is what love produces. It is love's nature. There is a sense in which God's Trinitarian family could not be contained; it had to expand and grow. Love had to continue to encompass more and more people. Creation is simply the expansion of God's family of love. This means that the "purpose" of creation is loving family. Humanity is meant to be part of God's Trinitarian life; we are intended to be children of God.

That is one aspect of what it means to be made in the image of God. Although this term encompasses attributes like rationality and sacredness and such, in the text it is primarily familial. For example, in Genesis 5:3 Adam fathered Seth "in his own likeness, in his own image." God gave us a different nature than the rest of creation in that we are his children, his offspring. God's goal in creating man was the creation of family. We will have more on this in chapter 14.

So we are made to love God and love one another. That is our ultimate purpose in life, and it is the end for which God works. As Jesus said, all the commandments are summed up in two lines: "Love the Lord your God with all your heart and with all your soul and with all your mind" and "Love your neighbor as yourself" (Matthew 22:37–39). Again, this is not arbitrary. Could the meaning of life have been any different? No, because God is love.

So how does this definition of love fit into our topic of worship and sacrifice? Why does God require people in the Old

Testament to sacrifice animals, and why does he constantly command humankind to worship him above all other things? In fact, this is so important to God that it is the focus of the first two commandments:

> You shall have no other gods before me. You shall not make for yourself an image in the form of anything in heaven above or on the earth beneath or in the waters below. You shall not bow down to them or worship them; for I, the LORD your God, am a jealous God, punishing the children for the sin of the parents to the third and fourth generation of those who hate me, but showing love to a thousand generations of those who love me and keep my commandments.
>
> Exodus 20:3–6

At first glance one can understand how this might make God appear petty and egotistical. However, as we examine this issue more closely, we will see that the truth is just the opposite. The fact is that God's desire for worship and sacrifice is intimately connected to his love for us. Love and sacrifice and worship are inseparable.

Love, Worship, and Sacrifice

To worship is to ascribe worth to something or someone. To sacrifice is to give up something. To love someone you must do both. Love and worship and sacrifice go together in that you generally love what you worship, and sacrifice is a part of both love and worship. I think we see this principle in our relationships every day.

For example, have you ever heard someone say, "He just worships the ground she walks on" or "She absolutely worships her husband"? These are good and proper sentiments. To say that

61

you "worship" your wife is to say that you ascribe great worth to her and are willing to do anything for her good. This is a sure sign of love.

We can also see this truth in potentially less commendable examples. If you hear that your friend "worships the Green Bay Packers" it may not cause too much alarm (because you think that hyperbole is being used), but if you hear that he is "worshiping money" or "worshiping alcohol" you probably should be concerned, especially if it is at the expense of his wife and children. Why? Because money and alcohol (and football, for that matter—in today's culture it may not be hyperbole) are not as valuable as one's family. It is wrong to ascribe more worth to stuff and sports than you do to your wife and kids because those things are not as objectively worthy as your family.

As such, if a man truly loves his wife and kids more than money and football and beer, he will give up those things if necessary. In other words, he will sacrifice those things if they get in the way of his family relationship.

The principle also applies to other aspects of family life. My wife and I have four children, and if getting married is like attending the college of "How to learn to sacrifice," then having kids is like going to graduate school. Parenting is all about sacrifice. From changing dirty diapers to paying for university, parents give of themselves for their children. Why do we do it? Because we love our kids. That is to say, we think our kids are far more valuable than anything else we are giving up for them. We worship them and are willing to sacrifice on their behalf. That is what love is.

So then, a major key to love is to only worship what is truly worthy and then to only ascribe the proper amount of worth to that thing or person. We need to keep our love ordered correctly. Some aspects of creation are worth more than others. Animals are worth more than rocks and humans are worth more than animals. We should not sacrifice the good of our child for the sake of the dog, for example. This is not arbitrary; it simply is the nature of reality. To ascribe more worth to a rock than to a person is to live contrary to the real world.

For example, if a man decided to sell his children into slavery for thirty pieces of gold, he would be doing the wrong thing not because of some arbitrary standard, but because his children are actually and objectively worth more than all the gold in the world.

Now, given that the purpose of life is love and that love is intimately tied to sacrifice and worship, we can accurately say that we were created for worship and sacrifice. Specifically, we were created to worship God and sacrifice to him.

Is God egotistical for desiring love and worship and sacrifice? Not at all, because he is worthy of them. Would we say that a wife is being egotistical for wanting her husband to love her and the kids more than football and alcohol? Absolutely not. She just wants him to live in accordance with the truth. The truth is that his family is much more important than those other things. To live contrary to reality simply doesn't work. It leads to nothing but trouble, like trying to run your gasoline-powered car with nothing but water in the fuel tank.

This is how we need to understand God's desire for sacrifice and worship. He did not create people in order to have his ego pumped up. He created us in order to have a reciprocal loving relationship with him. He wants to love and be loved. God is not an arbitrary egomaniac for desiring people to value him above all else. The simple fact is that God is worth more than anything else. To keep our relationship with him in tune with reality, we need to ascribe more worth to him than anything else. To not do so is to turn reality on its head, which always causes problems.

The Meaning of Life

We exist to love God and love each other. That is our ultimate purpose in life, and it is the end for which God works. We talked earlier about how the first two commandments involve worshiping nothing ahead of God. Now we see why. It's all about love. As we already noted, Jesus taught that all the commandments are summed up in two lines: "Love the Lord your God with all your heart and with all your soul and with all your mind" and "Love your neighbor as yourself" (Matthew 22:37–38).

Given that the purpose of life is love and to love is to give of ourselves for the good of others, we can accurately say that we were created for sacrifice. We were designed to give of ourselves for others. At its core, sin is a refusal to do that. To sin is to live out of tune with reality. Sin is a refusal to offer your worship and sacrifice to the proper being, God, and instead offer it to something or someone else. Humankind's fall was and is a failure to love.

In the garden of Eden, Adam and Eve saw that the fruit "was good for food and pleasing to the eye, and also desirable for gaining wisdom" (Genesis 3:6), and they decided that they wanted those things more than God. They would not sacrifice temporal, worldly benefit for eternal relationship with God. They decided to worship and serve the created thing rather than the creator, which is what we all do (Romans 1:23–25). Practically speaking, we value ourselves and our earthly pleasure above all and, as a result, are unwilling to give it up for God or anyone else. A good picture of humanity's base sin is the story of Esau, who sold his birthright for a bowl of food (Genesis 25:34). We refuse to love who we are meant to love, the one that is truly worthy of our love, and therefore our proper inheritance within his family is squandered. That is our foundational problem.

What God needs to do, then, is teach us to love.

Learning to Love

Again, family life gives us a good picture of this process. Children are not naturally self-giving. Quite the opposite, in fact; they are born with a penchant for pride and selfishness. They have to learn to love.

From my experience, I think this happens primarily in two ways: (1) by example and (2) through rules. I have wonderful parents, and I grew up watching them give and give and give for others. They dedicated their lives to their children and to the spreading of the gospel, and I have tried to model their example. As I do, I realize that they are the ones who showed me what it is to love. However, it wasn't just their example. They also had rules. My sisters and I weren't given optional guidelines about how to play together or divide our toys: We were forced to share. I am very thankful for that now, and I enforce the same rules on my kids. Either they share their toys—and every now and then give some away to kids who don't have any—or they don't get to play with them. In this way, I am trying to guide my children toward being loving people. I don't want them to grow up to be self-centered, egotistical brats. More specifically, I don't want them to grow up valuing themselves or their toys and games more than their siblings. One of the main reasons for forcing kids to share is to get it in their heads that other people are more important than toys, and that we should value the other person's experience more than our own. By forcing children to give up some time with the doll or the race car, I am trying to help them see that the other person is more important than either of those items, as fun as those things may be.

God uses the same type of techniques to teach us how to love: (1) He demonstrates love to us by sacrificing for us, and (2) he puts rules in place that are intended to push us toward placing the proper value on things. That is where all the rules about sacrifice come in. They are intended to teach us to love God and break us from our love for everything that is not God. Sacrifice is not commanded because God *needs* what we have. Sacrifice is commanded because of *our need* to give what we have to him. We can see clearly how this works in the Exodus story.

Sacrifice and the Exodus

The requirement to sacrifice was the original reason the Israelites were to leave Egypt. When Moses told Pharaoh to let God's people go, he explained that it was so the Hebrews could offer sacrifices in the desert (Exodus 7:16). After the plague of flies, Pharaoh said he would allow the Israelites to worship, but only within the land of Egypt. Moses refused the offer, explaining that the sacrifices that the Israelites were going to offer would be detestable to the Egyptians and cause an attack on the Israelites (Exodus 8:25–26). Why would the sacrifices of the Israelites be detestable to the Egyptians? Because the Hebrews were going to be sacrificing animals that the Egyptians venerated.

Egypt was a land of many gods, somewhat similar to India today. And like modern India, certain animals were considered holy. I have traveled to India several times, and one of the first things you notice is that cattle have a lot of freedom to roam. That is because in Hinduism, cattle (and other animals) are considered holy. Because of this, when I am in India, I do not suggest to the people that we lasso a wandering cow and slaughter it for the evening meal. That is the principle that Moses is applying here. He does not want to sacrifice within sight of the Egyptians, because he knows they would be highly offended because the animals being sacrificed are holy to them.

Why would God command the Israelites to sacrifice animals that were worshiped by the Egyptians? Because the Israelites were worshiping them too, and God wanted to break them of their idolatry! Israel had turned away from the one true God to worship foreign powers, and now God was attempting to bring them back to him. (See Joshua 24:14–18, 1 Samuel 12, and Exodus 20:7 for explicit references to the fact that the Israelites were idolaters in Egypt.) By commanding the Hebrews to sacrifice the animals that they had previously worshiped, God was (1) showing them that those beasts were not true gods, and (2) placing them in a position where they had to give up what was less valuable for what was more valuable. Sacrificing the animals to the one true God put them back in touch with reality; it ordered the universe correctly. God commanded the Israelites to sacrifice because he wanted them to renounce the Egyptian idolatry to which they were attached. This can also be deduced from several episodes in their subsequent wilderness journey.

For instance, soon after crossing the Red Sea, the Israelites complained because they had nothing to eat, and God graciously provided them with manna (Exodus 16:1–5). Interestingly, in Exodus 12:28 it says that the Israelites left Egypt with large herds and flocks. Why were they not eating the cattle and sheep? Could it be that they refused to kill them due to the fact that they still considered them holy?

That thesis becomes all the more reasonable when we consider later incidents, such as the building of the golden calf. Moses had given the people the Ten Commandments, the first two of which, remember, are "You shall have no other gods before me" and "You shall not make for yourself an image in the form of anything in heaven above or on the earth beneath or in the waters below" (Exodus 20:3–4). The people readily agreed to these rules, but before their vow of obedience had finished echoing around the desert floor, they were back to worshiping Egyptian idols! While Moses was back up on Mount Sinai, the people convinced Aaron to form for them an idol of gold, which they proceeded to worship (Exodus 32). Many scholars believe this calf represented the Egyptian god Apis. The people had come out of Egypt, but God had not yet got Egypt out of his people.

So what did God do? He gave them specific and mandatory rules for sacrifices that addressed their penchant for worshiping something other than God.

We see an example of this in the instructions for the Day of Atonement. Aaron the high priest was told to make two sin offerings: a young bull for himself (Leviticus 16:6, 11) and two goats and a ram for the people (Leviticus 16:5). The calf for Aaron makes sense because of the golden calf incident. God is specifically making a point to Aaron about worshiping cattle. But what about the requirement of goats for the rest? We see in the next chapter that God commands the people to stop worshiping "goat idols" or "goat demons" (Leviticus 17:7). It seems that while Moses was teaching the priestly code to the Levites for twelve weeks (the first half of Leviticus), the people were making offerings to some kind of goat idols. While the sacrifice of a goat at Yom Kippur was for all sins (Leviticus 16:16), it would have sent a specific message to the people at the time about not venerating goats.

God's commands about sacrifice were meant to break the people of their love for false gods and lead them to love the one true God. They were to give up something specific that they valued for the sake of someone they should value more. God didn't ask them to sacrifice ants or something else they didn't care about. He wanted them to give up the animal idols they were worshiping.

Again, this is a common principle in relationships. It means nothing to sacrifice something that you don't value. I have a friend who recently gave up watching basketball so he could spend more time with his wife. This is an act of love. However, it wouldn't have been an act of love to give up going to the opera for his wife, because he doesn't enjoy going to the opera anyway. He had to give up something that he valued, basketball, for it to be a truly loving gesture.

As we discussed above, sin is the refusal to love God and to accept his love. It is the refusal to sacrifice to him and to receive his sacrifice. The commandments were given to help reverse that situation. We need to understand, then, that God's interest in asking for sacrifice is part of his overall plan to get us to love him more than something or someone else. Although this is similar to my friend's basketball situation, it is far more serious: God's commands to Israel were like one spouse asking the other to stop cheating with prostitutes. To God, idolatry is adultery. In fact, that is just the language God uses in many places, including Judges 2:17, 8:27, and 1 Chronicles 5:25.

What does this mean to us today? We no longer have to sacrifice animals, but the principle of sacrificing as an act of love still applies. In fact, because of Jesus' example of perfect submission and obedience in giving himself to the Father (Philippians 2:1–11)—doing what the first Adam failed to do—we now see clearly what those sacrifices were supposed to lead us to: presenting ourselves as living sacrifices to God (Romans 12:1). Sacrifice was never about God needing animals. It was about breaking down barriers between humankind and God, whatever those barriers may be. Sacrificing ourselves to God means that we must give up anything and everything that might get in the way of our relationship with him.

Jesus exhibited this principle consistently in his ministry, starting with the first disciples:

As Jesus was walking beside the Sea of Galilee, he saw two brothers, Simon called Peter and his brother Andrew. They were casting a net into the lake, for they were fishermen. "Come, follow me," Jesus said, "and I will send you out to fish for people." At once they left their nets and followed him. Going on from there, he saw two other brothers, James son of Zebedee and his brother John. They were in a boat with their father Zebedee, preparing their nets. Jesus called them, and immediately they left the boat and their father and followed him.

Matthew 4:18–22

Peter, Andrew, James, and John left their nets and their families in order to follow Jesus. That is no small commitment. Why would Jesus ask them to do that? Because even the blessings of a job and family can become idolatrous. They can keep us from God. I have been saddened several times in my life by stories of young people who want to become missionaries or work in ministry or study theology but are thwarted at every turn by parents who want them to do something more "success-oriented" with their lives. It is frustrating to think that one's family could come between you and God, but that is exactly what Jesus said would happen:

> Do not suppose that I have come to bring peace to the earth. I did not come to bring peace, but a sword. For I have come to turn 'a man against his father, a daughter against her mother, a daughter-in-law against her mother-in-law—a man's enemies will be the members of his own household.'
>
> Anyone who loves their father or mother more than me is not worthy of me; anyone who loves his son or daughter more than me is not worthy of me. Whoever does not take up their cross and follow me is not worthy of me. Whoever finds their life will lose it, and whoever loses their life for my sake will find it.
>
> Matthew 10:34–39

Notice that Jesus frames the issue as one of love. Whoever does not give up everything—including his family—is showing that they love this world more than they love God. Loving God is necessary for eternal life:

> Anyone who loves their life will lose it, while anyone who hates their life in this world will keep it for eternal life. Whoever serves me must follow me; and where I am, my servant also will be. My Father will honor the one who serves me.
>
> John 12:25–26

This is the same point Jesus made to the wealthy young ruler when he asked what he needed to do to inherit eternal life. Jesus told him to "sell everything you have and give to the poor, and you will have treasure in heaven. Then come, follow me" (Luke 18:22). The man refused, and Jesus warned that having money makes it very difficult to enter the kingdom of God. The disciples were astonished at this, and Peter, perhaps wanting to confirm that he was not on the same track as the young ruler, blurted out, "We have left all we had to follow you!" (Luke 18:28). Jesus reassured him:

> Truly I tell you, no one who has left home or wife or brothers or sisters or parents or children for the sake of the kingdom of God will fail to receive many times as much in this age, and in the age to come eternal life.
>
> Luke 18:29–30

Those who love God will live forever with him. Those who do not will miss out on this blessing. The willingness to sacrifice is a clear sign of which side of that dividing line one is on.

God doesn't want only certain parts of our lives; for example, a tithe and a couple of hours on Sunday morning. He wants all of us. Therefore, he will ask us to sacrifice specific things that are (or might become) idolatrous to us. It's not going to be the same for every person. He might ask us for money, time, alcohol, the Internet, a boyfriend or girlfriend, or in my experience, a job and proximity to family.

In my early twenties I faced what was easily the biggest decision of my life to that point: Should I move from Canada to California to attend Bible college and work with an inner-city mission agency? I had recently become serious about following Jesus and was quite convinced that God wanted me to go. Although I was extremely excited about it, moving away from friends and family is never easy, and I struggled for a long time over what to do. At last, I settled on my course: off to California! Interestingly, just after making my decision, something came up that caused me to reconsider. Out of nowhere, I was offered a job on the oil rigs of northern Alberta. Money was scarce at the time, and this represented a chance to make some really good cash. What should I do? I must admit, I was very tempted to stay in Canada and work. However, after much prayer and thought, I decided to give up the high-paying job and go ahead and move. Looking back, it was definitely the right thing to do, and I have never regretted my decision. Since that time, I have had many similar experiences, all of which have reinforced for me the lesson I learned way back then: Relationship with God requires sacrifice.

The person you are trying to reach may see the sacrifices required by God in the Bible as evidence that he is a bloodthirsty tyrant bent on getting his pound of flesh from wherever he can. However, we have seen that sacrifice has been integral to God's relationship with the human race since the very beginning and continues to be so today. While we don't have to sacrifice animals anymore, God has not changed and the purposes for which God requires sacrifice have not changed. It's all about love.

The Reason for the Rules

Mishandling the Rules

It was one of the most exciting moments in young Ashly Erickson's life. As the freshman first baseman for Central Lakes College, she had just hit a home run in the bottom of the seventh inning to break a 0–0 tie and give her team the 2009 Minnesota College Athletic Conference women's softball championship. As she rounded third base several of her teammates, gripped by the euphoria of the moment, rushed out and gave her some high fives. That was the beginning of the end of the celebration. When Erickson touched home plate, the other team began shouting, "That's an out! She's out!" The opposing coach then informed the umpire of the rule that states teammates are not allowed to "touch a batter or base runner legally running the bases." The umpire listened, shrugged, and called Erickson out. The game went into extra innings and, as you might have guessed, Central Lakes went on to lose 4–0. As ESPN columnist Rick

Reilly recounts, "It was a walk-off-walk-back-on homer—the first game ever lost by congratulations." Reilly goes on:

> I hate this kind of crap. There's nothing cheaper than using some tiny, unconnected technicality to rob somebody of her rightful moment of glory, won fair and square. It's the cheapest thing in sports: an adult pencil-whipping some kid just because she can. And my e-mail box fills up with these kinds of stories all the time:
>
> *I lost the pine box derby because a den master said I didn't fill out the form right.*
>
> *They DQ'd our team because the coach found out I failed math class two years ago.*
>
> *They said the goal didn't count because my jersey was out.*
>
> Makes me want to chew a hole through my desk.[1]

I think we can all understand Reilly's frustration. He is rightly angry at people who either create silly and vindictive rules or misuse rules in a silly and vindictive way, a way they were never intended to be used. For example, I suspect the rule against touching base runners was intended to stop teammates from giving each other any sort of unfair advantage over the other team. Fast players aren't allowed to carry slow players around the bases, for instance. High-fiving a player who has already hit a home run offers no unfair advantage. While the letter of the law may have been violated by the congratulatory hand slap, the spirit certainly wasn't. The rule was used for a purpose for which it was never intended. I doubt that the author of that particular injunction would have considered the coach and her players "good sports" just because they followed the regulation.

Unfortunately, this approach to rules is not confined to sports. In an all-too-familiar story, five-year-old Liam Adams was recently suspended for three days from his kindergarten class at Cheviot Elementary in Cincinnati for violating the rule forbidding "possessing a dangerous weapon or object."[2] The problem is that he didn't possess a dangerous weapon or object at all. He brought a tiny plastic toy gun to school. It wasn't a threat to anyone or anything. I think we all realize why schools have anti-gun rules: They are intended to keep kids safe. Why, then, was little Liam suspended? Because some administrator didn't use the rule for its proper purpose. They followed the law as if the rules are good for their own sake. In this skewed view, sending a five-year-old home for having a toy pistol in his backpack is laudable for the simple reason that the rule was enforced.

I tell these sad stories because many skeptics view God in the way that Rick Reilly views the coach of the team that took away Ashly Erickson's home run. They see God as a "pencil-whipping" adult who enforces silly and vindictive rules on us in an attempt to spoil our enjoyment of life and just because he can.

If there is one aspect of the Bible story the skeptics you talk to are likely to know, it is the fact that God hands down rules from on high. However, they won't view the giving of this law as an act of grace, as the psalmist did (Psalm 119). Rather, they will probably understand the Ten Commandments (and the rest of the 613 rules in the Old Testament) as the edicts of a dictatorial taskmaster who loves to force people to jump through ridiculous hoops. For example, Christopher Hitchens speaks of God's actions at Sinai as the work of an authoritarian ruler that resulted in tyranny.[3]

The foundational problem with this position is that it only sees the letter of the law and not the spirit. This view understands the law as an end in and of itself rather than a means to a different end. In other words, these skeptics think that the rules themselves are what God considers righteous. Those who obey, then, are by definition good. Righteousness becomes "doing the right things" and "not doing the wrong things." A godly Christian is one who observes the rules.

For example, within this understanding of the law, I could put the Ten Commandments up on my wall and read them every night to evaluate how I've done that day. Did I murder anyone today? Nope. Check. Did I steal? Not a thing. Check. Did I have sex with anyone other than my wife? Negative. Check. Did I make or worship any statues? Not that I remember. Check. And on down the line. As long as I can check off everything (or at least most things) on the list of rules, I must be pretty righteous, right?

Wrong. The law is not an end in and of itself. It cannot be used as a checklist for measuring holiness. Rather, the law is a means to a different end: godly character. The rules are not intended to be an indicator of true holiness; they are designed to lead us to true holiness. To be truly righteous is to be a particular type of person. It is to exhibit certain inner character qualities. Being actually good according to God is not just about keeping the rules.

Adding Rules Upon Rules

Unfortunately, using commandments as a checklist for righteousness is very common among believers, so it is easy to see why skeptics would misunderstand the law. One reason so many people use the rules as a checklist is that it offers a straightforward and easy way of not only gauging one's moral worthiness, but of making oneself appear and feel more and more righteous. This is done by adding to the list and keeping more commandments than are even in the Bible!

For instance, every church subculture seems to have many extra-biblical rules (written or unwritten) that people follow. "Come to church a certain number of times per week"; "Serve in some capacity, such as teaching Sunday school"; "Wear a certain type of clothing"; "Listen to a particular style of music"; "Don't drink or smoke"; and so on. I once visited a church that had every congregant's name on a list in the foyer. Beside each name was a row of boxes to check, each representing an activity that the people were to have taken part in the previous week. Did you read your Bible twice a day? Check. Did you evangelize at least five people this week? Check. These things were seen as signs of righteousness, even though they are not explicitly commanded by God anywhere. However, they do provide an easy way to quantify whether or not you are a good person. "Why, I am an elder of the church board, give eleven percent of my income, and told twenty people about God last week, for goodness' sake. How much more holy can I get?"

Redefining the Rules

Treating the rules as a yardstick for holiness is also popular because it makes it easy to interpret the law in such a way as to allow for stuff that we want to do. So if the law teaches that I am not to gossip or lie about my neighbor, I can say, "Well, I didn't lie and gossip about my neighbor—the person I was talking about lives two doors down." A lot of teenagers I know have very explicit physical relationships with their boyfriends and girlfriends yet believe that they are doing nothing wrong because they didn't actually have intercourse. They define fornication in such a way that they can have sex without actually having sex. Convenient isn't it?

Hitchens rightly mocks this weasel-like approach to the rules, which he claims is prevalent among most religions. For example, he writes that Talmudic Judaism teaches:

> Don't do any work on the Sabbath yourself, but pay someone else to do it. You obeyed the letter of the law; who's counting?

The Dalai Lama tells us that you can visit a prostitute as long as someone else pays her. Shia Muslims offer "temporary marriage," selling men the permission to take a wife for an hour or two with the usual vows and then divorce her when they are done.[4]

Hitchens concludes from these observations that the god of these religions would rather have "hypocritical and self-interested affectation of faith"[5] than sincerity of heart, even sincere unbelief. In other words, Hitchens thinks the god of these religions is a tyrant because he is interested in an outward show of religious observations rather than a person's inner heart condition. In this view, God would rather have the softball game lost over high fives than won by a legitimate home run hit by an excitable freshman. If Hitchens is correct, he has a point.

Being, Not Doing

But he is not correct, at least in regard to Christianity. The answer to Hitchens' objection is that the God of the Bible evaluates these legalistic approaches to the law in the same way that Hitchens does. God also hates it and finds the hypocrisy of people who practice it appalling. There may be many who approach the rules as a benchmark of righteousness, but according to Christianity they are simply wrong, and skeptics are right to react negatively to it.

Instead of a standard for righteousness, God's law should be seen as a means to that end. It is a tool with a threefold purpose: It is pedagogical, protective, and punitive. In other words, it teaches, it shields from harm, and it acts as a punishment for doing evil. In all of these roles the rules are intended to guide a person toward true righteousness. True righteousness is about possessing the character qualities of God. One does not become righteous simply by keeping those rules or any of the other regulations we come up with. Rather, we become righteous as we mature and develop godly virtues. Holiness is not about *doing* certain things; it is about *being*—being like Christ.

A Parental Approach to the Rules

My wife and I have a list of rules for our children. For example, they are not allowed to hit each other, they have to wash their hands before meals, and they must say "please" and "thank you" at the appropriate times. We have several reasons for these rules, including our desire to keep them safe from harm and diseases and to be relationally skilled. However, we are not at all interested in having the children grow up to be self-aware of how polite, clean, or socially adept they are. In other words, these rules are not to be used as an end in themselves. They are a means to a different end. My wife and I don't want the kids to keep the rules for the sake of keeping the rules. They are meant to help lead them to develop certain good character and personality qualities; they are not indicators of those good qualities. If you have ever seen a child say "please" or "thank you" begrudgingly, you know how this truth plays out. The kid might say the right words, but that doesn't mean he is actually polite or thankful.

If our daughter didn't use the rules properly, she might grow up and think to herself, "I am such a cultured person. Look at how well-mannered and groomed I am. I am so thankful I had the proper upbringing." That is just the opposite of what we want. These rules are in place to keep our kids humble, not make them proud. We want them to say "please" as a sign of respect and "thank you" as a sign of gratitude. The rule is designed to point their attention away from themselves and toward the person they are addressing. To use the rule to pat themselves on the back is exactly the opposite of its intended use.

While we strictly enforce the rule about not hitting, it is not a license for the kids to pinch. ("But I didn't *hit* her!") It is also not an indication that we want the children to cease touching each other at all. ("You said I can't hit so I am never going to hug her again either!") We want the interpersonal relationship rules to guide the children toward actually caring about the well-being of their siblings. In the same way, personal hygiene rules are intended to engender a respect for one's body and a desire for healthy living. The heart condition is what is ultimately important; the rules are primarily a means to that end.

The Fulfillment of the Law

This is God's approach to the rules as well, as Jesus explained in his famous discourse the Sermon on the Mount. Just as God gave the people the Ten Commandments from a mountain, Jesus climbed one to explain those rules more clearly (Matthew 5–7). He started with the sixth commandment:

> You have heard that it was said to the people long ago, "You shall not murder, and anyone who murders will be subject to judgment." But I tell you that anyone who is angry with a brother or sister will be subject to judgment. Again, anyone who says to his brother or sister, "Raca," is answerable to the court. And anyone who says, "You fool!" will be in danger of the fire of hell.
>
> Matthew 5:21–22

Not only are we not to kill one another, Jesus says, but we are not even supposed to get angry with each other. We can't go to the rule list at the end of the day and check off number six and think we are doing all right. Instead of asking, "Did I kill anyone today?" we have to ask, "What was my attitude toward other people today?" This gets to the heart of the issue. God doesn't only want to keep you from murdering someone; he wants you to be a forgiving, loving person. God desires a heart condition that is not quantifiable. The rule about murder is to be followed, but it is not the end of the issue. Rather, it is a means to a further end. That end is a pure heart.

Jesus continued: "You have heard that it was said, 'You shall not commit adultery.' But I tell you that anyone who looks at a woman lustfully has already committed adultery with her in his heart" (Matthew 5:27–28). Jesus says it is not enough not to have sex with someone who is not your spouse. You are not even to lust after someone. You are to be a faithful person in your heart. You are to use the law to develop a character quality, not treat it as a task to be checked off.

The Old Testament law was given to the world for the same reason rules are given to children: to lead them toward righteousness of the heart. The rules are to be kept, but are not the end-all and be-all of righteousness. Character is. The rules are for children. When children grow up, they should no longer need the rules to tell them what to do. Rather, they should be the kind of people that the rules meant for them to be. For example, if my child who is now four continues to say her prayers and say "please" and "thank you" only out of obedience to me when she is twenty-five, there is a problem. By that time she should be mature enough, humble enough, and thankful enough to do those things because they flow naturally from who she is. I don't expect my son, who is now a toddler, to have to call me up when he is thirty to ask me how he should treat a co-worker who won't share. He should be well beyond that. That is the point: Rules are necessary for the immature, but as a person grows, he shouldn't need the rules anymore. The rules should have served their purpose and become superfluous. That is how God uses the rules as well. They are meant to lead us to being people of character.

Paul sums up this principle well and provides us with a nice list of qualities in Galatians 5: "The fruit of the Spirit is love, joy, peace, forbearance, kindness, goodness, faithfulness, gentleness and self-control. Against such things there is no law" (vv. 22–23). Notice that the fruit of the Spirit consists entirely of character qualities. Also, look how Paul ends the list: Against such things there is no law! Why is there no law? Because the law is for those who have not yet developed character qualities. The rules are for children, for the immature. When one grows up, the law is no longer needed.

That was largely Jesus' point to the Pharisees and other religious leaders of his day. They were the experts on the law, and as such should have realized that it was provisional. Instead, they treated it as the very embodiment of righteousness. Again and again Jesus scolded them with this passage, providing a good summary of his points:

> Woe to you, teachers of the law and Pharisees, you hypocrites! You give a tenth of your spices—mint, dill and cumin. But you have neglected the more important matters of the law—justice, mercy and faithfulness. You should have practiced the latter, without neglecting the former. You blind guides! You strain out a gnat but swallow a camel.
>
> Woe to you, teachers of the law and Pharisees, you hypocrites! You clean the outside of the cup and dish, but inside they are full of greed and self-indulgence. Blind Pharisee! First clean the inside of the cup and dish, and then the outside also will be clean.
>
> Woe to you, teachers of the law and Pharisees, you hypocrites! You are like whitewashed tombs, which look beautiful on the outside but on the inside are full of the bones of the dead and

everything unclean. In the same way, on the outside you appear to people as righteous but on the inside you are full of hypocrisy and wickedness.

Matthew 23:23–28

It doesn't get any clearer than that. Righteousness is not keeping the letter of the law in an outward show of obedience; it is a heart condition. Righteousness is qualitative, not quantitative. The Pharisees were very good at checking items off their daily list of rules and duties, but they missed the point. Notice that Jesus tells them they have "neglected the more important matter of the law—justice, mercy and faithfulness." This is just what we have been saying. God wants us to be a certain type of person: one that is just and merciful and faithful. God explains in Hosea 6:6: "I desire mercy, not sacrifice, and acknowledgment of God rather than burnt offerings." God does not need a percentage of our possessions as if that offering were good in and of itself. He desires that we be righteous on the inside. The Pharisaical approach to the law is exactly what Christopher Hitchens was talking about when he criticized the practice of paying others to work on the Sabbath. It turns out that Hitchens was exactly right. What he failed to realize is that Jesus beat him to the punch by about two millennia. God does not hand down rules just for the sake of watching us jump through hoops. Rather, he gives us the rules because he is interested in making us into the type of people who can live forever in familial communion with him. His goal is to make us mature adults.

The Unity of God's Work

Clarifying the reason for the rules will help the skeptic understand the relationship between the law and true righteousness.

It will also help him see the unity of God's overall plan. Often unbelievers are confused by the fact that there are some rules we don't follow anymore (such as Sabbath keeping), and that God seems to allow things in the Old Testament that he no longer finds acceptable in the new. For example, earlier I mentioned a listener named Justin who sent me an email asking why God wasn't more concerned about slavery in the Old Testament. Part of my answer to Justin was that God had to accommodate the people in the moral condition they were in. It's not that God wasn't concerned about slavery; it's that he was dealing with cultures that were morally immature. He implemented laws that were pedagogical, protective, and punitive within the context of their situation. For example, one part of the law prescribed taking "an eye for an eye" (Exodus 21:24). Today this rule is viewed by most people in the West as barbaric. However, compared to taking the life of an entire family, just taking another person's eye is quite an improvement. The law was, in fact, a move toward civility in ancient Near-Eastern culture. "An eye for an eye" was not yet "Love your enemy," but as Jesus explained (Matthew 5:38–42), its purpose was to move the people in that direction.

While it may seem to skeptics that God is inconsistent in the way he deals with people, the fact is that he is entirely consistent, but he is dealing with real people, not computer programs. He can't just flip a switch or rewrite a line of code and make people instantly hate slavery or treat their neighbors with humility and love. He needs to relate to people in the immature state they are in and attempt to grow them up. This takes time and various means. So although it may look like God is changing the rules, in fact he is simply accommodating people in various cultures at various stages of history while keeping the overarching goal the same.

I applied the principle of accommodation when I worked for five years with inner-city youth. Part of our ministry involved taking kids from troubled backgrounds to the mountains for summer camp. Well, let's just say that many of the youngsters I was in charge of at camp operated according to a different value system than that with which I had been raised. Hard street life was all they had ever known. Therefore, it was simply not realistic to expect them to behave like I did as a kid or like my own children do. Most of the urban youth simply weren't spiritually or morally mature enough to do that.

As such, I adjusted my rules accordingly. For example, I gave junior high boys rules about hitting and stealing that my own son had mastered by the age of three. Rather than expect them to love their enemies, I tried to make them less dangerous to their enemies as a step toward that more distant goal. I also was much more lenient with my camp kids in regard to crude and vulgar language than I am with my children at home. Does that mean I wanted the inner-city youth to be foul-mouthed? Of course not, but I had to deal with reality. They simply were not going to be able to instantly and completely change the way they talked.

Now, if someone looked at the way I interacted with my camp kids compared to the way I parented my own children, they might say that I was inconsistent. Shouldn't I have the same rules for both groups? The answer is no, and it's not because I am inconsistent. The difference is not in me, but the kids. Rules that I implemented at camp would be completely unnecessary at home because the purpose of those rules had already been accomplished there.

As we have seen, this is what Jesus and Paul and the rest of the New Testament writers taught concerning the law. God was dealing with people where he found them. That is not to say he was content to leave them there. However, he had to deal with reality. He gave them rules pertaining to their situation and even condescended to allow them certain practices that he was not in favor of due to the hardness of their hearts. For example, Moses allowed the people to divorce as a protective measure for the women. Allowing an official divorce was better than having an unwanted wife turned out on her own, or worse. However, as Jesus explained, God has never approved of divorce. His allowance of it was strictly due to the immature state of the people (Matthew 19:7–9).

Conclusion

In the previous chapter I argued that the meaning of life is to love God and that he requires worship and sacrifice as a means to that end. In this chapter we talked about why God gave us the rest of the rules. Ultimately, they are given for the same purpose, because to love God is to enter into the blessed life of the Trinity, and that is only available to those who become like God. In other words, a relationship with God is not for those who just keep the letter of the law, but for those who actually become godly.

///////////// **6**

What Jesus Meant by That Whole "Born Again" Thing

Thinking Like a Child

I clearly remember the moment I became a Christian. I don't recall how old I was exactly, probably six or seven, but it was a Sunday afternoon and I had been to church that morning. Something about Sunday school must have made an impression on me, because I asked my mother to come to my room to talk to me about getting saved. She graciously led me in a prayer of repentance and faith, and as we finished, I felt great joy and relief sweep over me. I knew that I was going to get into heaven because Jesus had died for me.

If you had asked me at the time what it meant to be "saved," I'm not sure what I would have told you. However, as I think back now to the theology of my youth, several images come to mind.

For one, I considered salvation as a type of fire insurance. To avoid hell, make sure you sign on the dotted line by doing whatever the preacher says you need to do (believe, repent, have faith, give your life to Jesus), and then rest easy, knowing that you are covered. Your papers are in order, and when that fateful day arrives, everything will be just fine.

Along the same lines, I thought that "getting saved" was like making a reservation at a very ritzy and exclusive club. As long as you have made that phone call at some point in your life, when you show up at the pearly gates, Saint Peter will see that your name is in the book and welcome you in!

In more familial and relational terms, I thought of becoming a child of God as a one-time transaction in which I got a new legal guardian, but one with whom I didn't get to live. It's like I was living in an orphanage but had to stay there, even though I was now assigned a new name and even guaranteed an inheritance at some point in the future.

This whole arrangement seemed to me a bit like a professional athlete getting traded from one franchise to another. When a player moves to a new team, he remains the same person. The organization that owns his contract changes and he puts on a different uniform for games, but Joe Football Star is still the same Joe on the inside. Fans generally don't care about the inside, though. Those who hated Joe when he played for the archrival will now cheer their hearts out for him when he takes the field for the home team, no matter what kind of person he is away from the stadium.

Practically speaking, I realize now that one of the main consequences of this theology was that I lived a spiritually pathetic life. By that I mean that I wasn't really any different from any of the unbelievers I knew. I was enslaved to the same sins, beset by the same character flaws, and guided by the same materialistic priorities as everyone else. However, this didn't really bother me much because I didn't think it mattered as far as my ultimate destination was concerned.

This is not to say that I just sinned rampantly and accepted every evil the world offered. I tried to live a reasonably good life in appreciation for what God had done for me. (And if I remember correctly, that was usually the reason given by pastors to motivate us to moral behavior.) But I didn't pursue a life of radical righteousness or intimacy with God, largely because I didn't think it was possible or consider it something God was all that interested in.

I don't remember ever being taught this explicitly, but the practical consequence of my view of salvation at the time is that "children of God" or "Christians" can stay essentially unchanged on the inside. That is exactly what I did, because I didn't think it mattered to God what my insides looked like anyway, at least not in relation to my salvation. God didn't take into account my sin and worldly ambition; he only saw the "Jesus covering" he had placed on me. I figured that I may not be actually righteous, but God saw me as legally righteous, so everything was all right.

I was certainly not alone in this. Indeed, many Christians today operate according to this theology of salvation. That is one reason why the morality of Christians is essentially the same as that of non-Christians.[1] Speaking of evangelicals in particular, but making a statement that is applicable across the Christian spectrum, Michael Horton laments: "Christians are as likely to embrace lifestyles every bit as hedonistic, materialistic, self-centered, and sexually immoral as the world in general."[2]

More Than a Onetime Legal Transaction

I now realize that my theology was wrong. In the previous two chapters I have argued that God is very concerned with making us into particular kinds of people. That is to say, he actually wants us to be holy and righteous on the inside. He wants us to be like Jesus.

In this chapter I want to drive that truth home with more force and clarity by showing how it applies to salvation and being a child of God. I am convinced that a major reason there are not more saints in the world is that most people think they can get into heaven without being one. They believe that as long as they have had their name checked as "forgiven," all will be well. They are wrong. Salvation involves much more than that.

As we will see, legal forgiveness is only one part of the equation. God doesn't just purchase sinners while leaving them essentially unchanged. He doesn't just take legal guardianship of children and cover their sins. Rather, he creates new children who are in intimate union with him. God doesn't just look at a believer as if she were a new person; she actually is a new person. The old person is dead; a new person is alive.

Becoming a Christian involves not the covering of the old but the destruction of the old. It is the annihilation of satanic powers and flesh that enslaved us and the creation of a new person who is as united to God as a biological child is to his parents, only more so. Becoming a Christian is to become a new baby in Christ. By its very nature, this is a life of ever-increasing holiness. My theology was missing these truths.

A Major Obstacle to Belief

The reason I bring this up in a book about evangelism is that my childhood beliefs regarding salvation, and the spiritually weak Christians it produces, are a huge stumbling block for skeptics.

Unbelievers simply can't abide the notion that, when it comes to salvation, God doesn't care what kind of person you are. They can't understand why God would forgive some people and let them into heaven ahead of those who have lived morally better lives based on something as seemingly capricious and silly as saying a prayer, intellectually assenting to certain propositions, getting confirmed, or jumping through an equally arbitrary hoop. For example, in the "An Atheist Meets God" video I mentioned earlier, the god character tells the unbeliever that he is going to burn in hell because he failed to believe the propositions written in a 2,000-year-old book even though he has admittedly lived a very moral life. It seems terribly unjust.

Frankly, if the view of salvation I presented above was correct, the skeptics would have valid concerns here. However, it isn't. These objections are based on a misunderstanding of God and his plan for the world.

A Pattern for Building a Family and Dealing With Sin

We have seen in the previous chapters that God's plan for humanity is to live in intimate union with him. Our purpose for living is to be part of God's family, but sin has resulted in a break in that relationship. In this section we will examine how God has worked in history to rebuild his family. As we survey that work briefly, we will see that God has a very consistent and quite explicit pattern for dealing with rebellion and disorder. God doesn't just declare guilty sinners "not guilty" or offer them forgiveness and a new legal status. He doesn't just put a coat of whitewash on a deformed planet and label it OKAY. Instead, he makes all things new. Indeed, creation as the solution to sin is one of the key themes in redemptive history.

To see how this theme has played out over time, we first need to realize that the context for the entire biblical narrative is one of a war between God and the forces of evil. This battle is described using many different metaphors: light versus darkness, chaos versus order, and slavery versus freedom, among others. In what follows I will make the case that God's means of winning this war is an act of new creation that destroys the enemy while at the same time bringing forth the new family of God led by one special man. The decisive action of God brings both judgment and new life.

It seems to me that we usually think of creation as a peaceful act; I envision a painter with his canvas or a sculptor with her clay, for instance. However, although God is certainly an artist, it is more biblical, at least in regard to our theology of salvation, to think of creation as an act of war, as a decisive blow to the enemy in a cosmic battle. This is apparent even from the first verses of Genesis.

The Creation of the Universe as the Defeat of Leviathan

According to Genesis 1, in the beginning there was formlessness, darkness, and water. Traditionally, this has been understood as a state of lifeless disorder. The Spirit of God hovers over the proceedings and, as the Spirit works, the Earth is gradually turned from a chaotic wasteland to a well-ordered planet brimming with life. Here we see the first instance in the Bible of an act of creation that brings judgment and new life at the same time.

The life-giving aspect of the creation story is obvious, as the Spirit draws life out of the water and we end up with not only plants and animals, but the crown of creation: God's first human children, Adam and Eve. They are the father and mother of the family of God on Earth. God has created descendants for himself.

The destructive part of the original creation is perhaps not so obvious to modern Western readers. However, theologians have long viewed the creation narrative as the story of God's victory over the sea dragon Leviathan, which represents death.[3] The sea symbolizes chaos and God's victory establishes order. This "cosmic battle" motif was well known to the ancient Israelites and is clearly displayed in several other places in Scripture. For

example, Psalm 104:7 describes the waters fleeing at God's rebuke, and in Psalm 89:9–10 we see God ruling over the surging
sea and crushing Rahab, another sea monster; in Job 9:13, the
"cohorts of Rahab cowered" at God's feet.[4]

As is clear in these passages, the ancient Israelites clearly
associated creation with victory over evil forces. Notice also that
the sea itself is representative in that culture of the evil forces
that God works to defeat. That is one of the reasons Jesus' calming the storm (Mark 4:35–41) was such a big deal, and why the
final act of creation, the new heaven and earth, will have no sea
(Revelation 21:1). But I am getting ahead of myself! For now I
just want to emphasize that the creation of the world involved
both bringing forth life and defeating death. Also, notice again
that this life is a family led by one special man. As we will see,
the exact same thing can be said about the great flood.

Noah and the Flood

Adam and Eve rebelled against God, and their descendants
became more and more evil (Genesis 3–4). God decided to act.
Interestingly, he did not give the people a quick and easy legal
way out. He did not offer them a free ticket to a future paradise
if they would believe some facts about him. He did not decide to
pick a few people and arbitrarily label them RIGHTEOUS rather
than SINFUL. Instead, he eradicated the evil and started all over
again. This was much more than a declaration. The Earth was
actually returned to the chaotic, watery, and dead state from
which it came, and then God created the world for a second time.
Noah was the second Adam, and the story of the fresh start his
family received is a second act of creation. I think we see this
clearly in the overall narrative, but also in some of the specific
literary clues and historical parallels between the two accounts.

For example, the flood begins when "the springs of the great deep burst forth" (Genesis 7:11). The word for *deep* is the same word used in Genesis 1:2 to describe the initial watery condition of the Earth.

Also, there is an emphasis on the number seven in the flood story: Noah is to take seven pairs of clean animals (Genesis 7:2); he is in the ark for seven days before the flood begins (Genesis 7:4), and a dove is sent every seven days to search for land (Genesis 8:10–12).

As for that dove, the fact that it hovers over the water is reminiscent of the Spirit hovering over the waters in Genesis 1. What is its goal? To bring life (in the form of a branch) out of the water.

Noah's relationship to Adam is made quite explicit in Genesis 9:1–2, where he is given dominion over the plants and animals and told to be fruitful and multiply. This, of course, is the role and command that God originally gave to Adam (Genesis 1:28). Noah was now the leader of God's family; he was the new Adam. Noah was the righteous man who would be the father of God's children. So the flood was a creative act that brought judgment on the sinful human race. At the flood, "the whole universe, soiled by the tide of sin, by the intervention of water was restored to its pristine purity"[5] and out of the water came a people of God, a new righteous line led by one special man.

Moses and the Crossing of the Red Sea

The Red Sea crossing was one more instance in which God re-created a family by using one special man to lead people through the water of destruction and out of it to new life. On one side of the water the Israelites were "dead": Although they were on the run, in a very real sense they still belonged to the Pharaoh and his army. However, on the other side they were newly "alive": The Pharaoh had been defeated and they were now a new people. God had defeated evil and created for himself (again) a son. Israel had been born again.

Before we delve more deeply into the drama at the Red Sea, let's set the stage by examining the account of the birth of that special man, Moses. I believe Moses' early childhood is the first aspect of the Exodus account that shows the connection between creation, the flood, and the Red Sea.

The man whom God would use to deliver his people was born under a death sentence. The Pharaoh had ordered that all male Hebrew babies should be killed by being thrown into the Nile River (Exodus 1:22). In the context of the narrative, the waters of the Nile are the waters of death and destruction.

Moses' mother protected him for three months, but when she could no longer hide him, she made a basket, put Moses in it, and placed it in the reeds along the bank of the Nile. At that time Pharaoh's daughter came down to the river to bathe, noticed the baby in the basket, and took him home to raise him as her own. She named him Moses, which means "I drew him out of the water" (Exodus 2:10).

So Moses was born in a similar situation to the people of Earth at the time of the flood: sentenced to death by water. However, Moses, like Noah before him, escaped that judgment by entering into an ark and thus came through the waters of destruction. Indeed, not only did Moses survive, but he was given a new life as a royal son. Moses entered into the water a slave but came out of it as a member of the Pharaoh's family! There is a very real sense in which Moses was born again in that water. That is why he was given his name. He had been re-created, given new life by being drawn out of the water. Indeed, from an Egyptian perspective (they believed the Pharaoh was a god), Moses had been given divine life.

Moses is like Noah and like Adam. He is the leader of a family of God. Where is this family created? I think it is clear that new life is given to the people of God at the Red Sea. Just like Moses, they are born again as they are drawn out of the water.

Let's examine this more closely. Like Moses, the Israelites were also in a similar position to the people of Earth before the flood: They were under penalty of death, part of a sinful culture that was under God's judgment. However, the link between the situation of the Israelites in slavery and humanity at the time of the flood is even more explicit in that the problems of the Israelites in Egypt are allegorically the problems of all humankind since the fall of Adam. They were (1) separated from their true home, (2) in slavery to the Pharaoh, and (3) under God's judgment for worshiping false gods. In the same way, the people before the flood were (1) separated from God, (2) in slavery to sin and Satan, and (3) under God's judgment for worshiping false gods. It is the same threefold problem we all face today, by the way.

The parallels between the Red Sea and the flood continue in the way the people were saved. Like those who followed Noah into the ark and through the water before them, the Israelites who followed Moses through the waters of the Red Sea were spared. The dry land appeared (as at the original creation), and the water that brought judgment and death to their Egyptian enemies was defeated. The Red Sea crossing was a creative act that destroyed evil. As such, it conformed perfectly to God's previously established pattern for dealing with sin.

Before moving on to how this pattern continues right up until our day, let's pause and point out again that God did not save his people by simply forgiving them. He gave them a new existence. God didn't just grant the people a cloak of righteousness; he took them through the water to make them a new, holy people.

This is not the end of the story of redemption, of course. Moses and the Israelites are types. They show us how God works and foreshadow his ultimate purpose, which is to create a spiritual and eternal family. He does this, as usual, through one special man.

By now I suspect that you can see where I am going with this: Jesus is like Moses in that he is the one who defeats death and leads us to new life. As we look briefly at a few of the parallels between Jesus and Moses, it should help us to better understand Jesus' mission and help equip us to be able to correct skeptics' misconceptions about salvation.

Similarities Between Moses and Jesus

The first similarity between Moses and Jesus involves the circumstances of their births. Moses was born into an oppressed people living under an evil tyrant who tried to have him killed. So was Jesus. Just like the Pharaoh centuries before him, King Herod was concerned about someone rising up to take his throne (Matthew 2:3–6). He heard that a "King of the Jews" had been born and, in order to quell an uprising before it started, he ordered that all male Hebrew babies two years old and younger in and around Bethlehem be killed (Matthew 2:16). Jesus' parents fled to Egypt, where they stayed until Herod died (Matthew 2:14–15).

Another aspect of Moses' life that points toward Jesus is the fact that he gave up his position of honor and privilege to identify with the people he loved. Moses was a powerful prince, but he humbled himself and became a shepherd, herding flocks in the middle of nowhere. The writer of Hebrews describes his action this way:

> By faith Moses, when he had grown up, refused to be known as the son of Pharaoh's daughter. He chose to be mistreated along with the people of God rather than to enjoy the fleeting pleasures of sin.
>
> Hebrews 11:24–25

In the same spirit as Moses, Jesus gave up his position in heaven in order to identify with the people he loved. Paul portrays Jesus in these glowing terms:

> Who, being in very nature God, did not consider equality with God something to be used to his own advantage; rather, he made himself nothing by taking the very nature of a servant, being made in human likeness. And being found in appearance as a man, he humbled himself and became obedient to death—even death on a cross!
>
> Philippians 2:6–8

Here is another similarity: When Moses came to lead his people, most didn't welcome him with open arms. Pharaoh responded to Moses' first demand to let the people go by making their work even harder, which resulted in the Hebrews cursing Moses for bringing more trouble on them (Exodus 5:19–21).

In the same way, Jesus was "despised and rejected by mankind, a man of suffering, and familiar with pain. Like one from whom people hide their faces he was despised, and we held him in low esteem" (Isaiah 53:3). John explains that "he came to that which was his own, but his own did not receive him" (John 1:11). Jesus came to set humanity free, but most people weren't interested. Rather than follow, they called for his crucifixion.

Dual Family Ties

Moses and Jesus had remarkably similar life experiences that should make us ponder the link between the two men. However, perhaps the strongest illustrative parallel between Moses and Jesus is the unique family ties that each possessed. Both Moses and Jesus were members of two families, one royal and one common, and these multiple connections were necessary to complete their redemptive missions.

As we discussed above, Moses was born a Jew but was adopted into the Egyptian ruling family. As a Hebrew he was able to relate to the people and exercise the authority necessary to lead them; it seems unlikely they would have followed a non-Israelite. On the other hand, as a member of Pharaoh's family, Moses was granted the access necessary to enter the court and demand the slaves' release. It seems unlikely that he would have been able to do this if he did not have that connection. Moses needed to be both an Egyptian royal and an Israelite to accomplish his task.

In the same way, Jesus is a man but is also God. He was born to Mary in Bethlehem, but at the same time has always existed as part of the Godhead (John 1:1). As a member of the human family, he is able to relate to us and exercise the necessary authority to lead us home. As the Son of God, Jesus has access to the very throne room of God, so that he may make intercession for us (Romans 8:34). The fact that he was both God and man was and is absolutely essential to his task.

God providentially placed Moses in Pharaoh's family so when the time was right, he would have access to the seat of power and secure the Jews' release. In this way, God illustrated what would later occur with Jesus.[6] Jesus is the one who has membership in the divine royal family necessary to save us.

Jesus, Baptism, and the Creation of a Spiritual People of God

This unique nature was dramatically proclaimed and illustrated in one of the more striking and beautiful scenes in the New Testament: Jesus' baptism by John in the Jordan River. When Jesus came up out of the water, the Spirit of God in the form of a dove descended and landed on him and a voice from heaven proclaimed, "This is my Son" (Matthew 3:17).

This is an amazing episode in that it brings together much of the imagery from this chapter. For example, the Spirit of God, descending in the form of a dove over the river, brings to mind both the initial creation account of the Spirit hovering over the water and the flood in which the dove also hovered over the water. As we discussed, in both cases the Spirit/dove brought life out of the water.

As for bringing life from the water, we have also seen that in each case God brought "divine" life out of the water. Moses was drawn out of the water to be part of the royal family, and in the other instances God brought entire groups out of the water to be part of his family. In the case of Jesus, he is God, a member of the Trinity. He was not made God at his baptism, but his status as God's Son was officially pronounced to the world at that time. Here we have the fulfillment of everything God had been working toward since the fall: the new Adam that all the other "Adams" had been pointing toward. With Jesus, God's plan for creating a new family of God through one special man finds fulfillment. A new righteous line has begun, one that is radically unlike the first. The main difference is that while the first Adam was physical, Jesus is a spiritual Adam:

> So it is written: "The first man Adam became a living being"; the last Adam, a life-giving spirit. The spiritual did not come first, but the natural, and after that the spiritual. The first man was of the dust of the earth; the second man is of heaven. As was the earthly man, so are those who are of the earth; and as is the heavenly man, so also are those who are of heaven. And just as we have borne the image of the earthly man, so shall we bear the image of the heavenly man.
>
> 1 Corinthians 15:45–49

Jesus has divine life and bears children that have divine life as well! Those who become a part of God's family are not simply forgiven or granted a new legal status, they are re-created.

That is why the entrance rite of the church has always been baptism. We enter the baptismal water under God's judgment and as slaves to sin and to Satan; we come out of it as free children of God. In fulfillment of the action of the flood and the Red Sea, our evil nature is destroyed in the water and we are granted new life. These connections between the flood, the Red Sea crossing, and baptism are explicitly made by Peter in 1 Peter 3:20–21 and by Paul in 1 Corinthians 10:1–2.

Living As New Creations

The point of this very brief historical survey of God's redemptive work is to emphasize that salvation involves God making us into new people, not just giving us a whitewash. When Jesus told Nicodemus that he must be born again to enter the kingdom of God (John 3:1–3), he actually meant it. He wasn't talking about giving Nicodemus new legal standing as a member of God's family. He wasn't talking about painting over Nicodemus the sinner with a "righteousness covering." Jesus actually meant that Nicodemus needed to be created again by God.

When I realized this, my attitude toward sin started to change. I could no longer accept living a mediocre life in which sin still largely had control. If God had made me new, I needed to start living like it. This is exactly Paul's point in much of his ethical teaching. He spends a lot of time in the beginning of his letters establishing the nature of our new identity, saying things like "If anyone is in Christ he is a new creation; the old has gone, the new has come!" (2 Corinthians 5:17 NIV1984). He then follows that with an exhortation to live accordingly. For example, this

passage from the first half of Ephesians establishes that we are
new creations:

> As for you, you were dead in your transgressions and sins, in
> which you used to live when you followed the ways of this world
> and of the ruler of the kingdom of the air, the spirit who is now
> at work in those who are disobedient. All of us also lived among
> them at one time, gratifying the cravings of our flesh and fol-
> lowing its desires and thoughts. Like the rest, we were by nature
> deserving of wrath. But because of his great love for us, God,
> who is rich in mercy, made us alive with Christ even when we
> were dead in transgressions—it is by grace you have been saved.
>
> Ephesians 2:1–5

We were dead and now we are alive! It reminds me of what the
father said about his prodigal son when he returned: "This son
of mine was dead and is alive again" (Luke 15:24). The implications of this truth are spelled out in the last half of Ephesians.
They include this instruction:

> You were taught, with regard to your former way of life, to
> put off your old self, which is being corrupted by its deceitful
> desires; to be made new in the attitude of your minds; and to
> put on the new self, created to be like God in true righteousness
> and holiness.
>
> Ephesians 4:22–24

So we are a new creation, one that is intended to actually be
righteous and holy. We simply cannot be satisfied with not being
so. If we are children of God, something really has changed
about us. It is not just a new label, but a new reality. When God
has children, he is not giving orphans new names or drafting
an expansion team, but actually creating brand-new children.
Richard White explains:

We are born with the nature of Adam and are thereby sinners. But Christ is the New Adam. When we are united to Him through grace, we are justified. Paul states, "For as by one man's disobedience many were *made sinners*, so by one man's obedience many will be *made righteous*" (Romans 5:19). Note that in Adam we are not just declared sinners, we are made sinners. By the same token, in Christ we are not just declared righteous but are made righteous. Our righteousness in Christ is not only legal but real, just as our sinfulness in Adam was not only legal but real.[7]

As we discussed in the previous chapter, God's ultimate intent is to have a family of mature adults, living together as the Trinity lives together. God's first step in that process is to create new life. The skeptics who recoil from a theology of salvation that focuses on legally renaming sinners while leaving them in their sin are right to do so. That has never been God's intention. Those Christians who think they are saved but bear no evidence of new life need to question whether they truly are children of God: "This is how we know who the children of God are and who the children of the devil are: Anyone who does not do what is right is not a child of God: nor is anyone who does not love his brother" (1 John 3:10 NIV1984).

Conclusion

Skeptics generally reject a view of salvation that is incomplete at best and just plain false at worst. We need to make them aware that salvation is not just forgiveness of sin, although that is part of it. It is not even only about freedom from sin, although that is part of it as well. Salvation is about being created anew as a child of God. Scott Hahn says it well:

Salvation is not only *from* sin, but *for* sonship—in Christ. We are not only forgiven by God's grace, we are adopted and divinized, that is, we "become partakers of the divine nature" (2 Peter 1:4). This is ultimately why God created us, to share in the life-giving love of the Trinity. Self-sacrificial love is the essential law of God's covenant, which we broke—but Jesus kept. After assuming our humanity, He transformed it into a perfect image—and instrument—of the Trinity's love, by offering a sacrificial gift-of-self to the Father on our behalf. The Son of God "took the form of a servant" (Philippians 2:7) so that sinful servants may be restored as sons of God. As Saint Athanasius declared: "The Son of God became the Son of Man so that sons of men could become sons of God."[8]

Why Hell Is Fair
and Heaven Won't Be Boring

Can the Existence of Hell Be Reconciled
With a Loving God?

My conversation partner was becoming agitated. I had been trying to explain that God's goal for humanity is to draw us into the life of the Trinity to live with him in loving relationship for eternity. In other words, I was presenting some of the material we covered in the previous three chapters of this book. The skeptic was not buying it. "How can you call God loving?" he exclaimed. "Would you call me loving if I locked my daughter in a dungeon and tortured her for not doing her homework? Would you call me loving if I imprisoned my wife in a room and then tormented her day and night for burning the toast?"

If there is one objection that is almost guaranteed to come up in a conversation about Christianity, this is it. Many people simply cannot reconcile the idea that God loves us but some people end up in hell. As James Lileks writes, "As a tot I was given the usual terrifying mixed message: (a) God is love; and (b) If you don't believe how much He loves you, you will stand in the corner for eternity."[1]

The first key to dealing with this objection is to admit that if hell is a place where an angry God tortures people for eternity just because they failed to believe the right propositions or meet some of his arbitrary standards for a few measly years here on Earth, it is unjust and we shouldn't label God loving. The god of Lileks' childhood memory *is* sending a terrifying mixed message. Unfortunately, this is the type of God that many Christians have been proclaiming for too long.

It is also the type of God the man I was talking to was rejecting. In speaking to people who have this view, I recommend that we first explain to them that we reject it as well. Then we have to provide a more accurate account of the afterlife. For example, here is how the rest of my conversation went.

"Of course I wouldn't say you were loving if you did those things," I replied. "But that is not analogous to God and hell. Now let me ask you something. Would you call yourself a loving husband if you cheated on your wife? Or would you call yourself a loving son if, assuming you had good parents, you rejected all that they had done for you and refused to acknowledge or speak to them? And would these decisions have inherent consequences? By that I mean, would your relationship with your wife and parents be affected by your attitudes and behavior?"

"Well, no, that wouldn't be loving, and yes, it would have consequences," the caller admitted.

"Of course," I said. "And that is the better picture of what happens between humans and God. Heaven and hell are not places of arbitrary rewards and punishments. Rather they are the state of existence that results as a natural consequence of either loving God or failing to do so."

I argued in chapter 4 that love is the most foundational truth in all of reality. In short, love is the meaning of life. We were made to give of ourselves for God and for others; it is inherent in our existence. I also suggested that reality is hierarchical. Certain parts of existence are more objectively valuable than other parts and we are to love according to that order. In other words, we are to love God above all and love everything else in keeping with its inherent value.

Sin is disordered love. It is to give of ourselves to (worship and serve) something or someone to a degree beyond which it is worthy. Such love carries with it its own inherent punishment (Romans 1). We probably all know people who have been sucked further and further into a particularly destructive pattern of life that ruins their relationships. For example, the man who worships and serves alcohol or money more than his wife and children is out of touch with reality and will bear the consequences of that decision.

The ultimate consequence of disordered love is the state of existence we call hell. The more we love things other than God, whether money or power or simply ourselves, the further away we get from the relationship for which we were created. In the same way that a husband will grow further and further away from his family as he continues to worship and serve other things, people grow further and further away from God. Eventually we are completely alone. That is hell.

People don't get sent to hell because they didn't believe the right things while on earth. They don't get rejected at the pearly gates because they failed to jump through the right hoops. They end up in a state of alienation from God because that is what happens when you don't love him. It's simply the nature of reality. Dallas Willard offers this good insight:

We should be very sure that the ruined soul is not one who has missed a few more or less important theological points and will flunk a theological examination at the end of life. Hell is not an "oops!" or a slip. One does not miss heaven by a hair, but by constant effort to avoid and escape God. "Outer darkness" is for one who, everything said, wants it, whose entire orientation has slowly and firmly set itself against God and therefore against how the universe actually is. It is for those who are disastrously in error about their own life and their place before God and man.[2]

The picture of God standing over hell gleefully throwing poor souls into the pit because they didn't measure up to his rules is simply false. People take themselves to hell. Regis Martin rightly notes:

Hell is the condition of man who, having habituated himself to a life of complete self-enclosure, announces forever before God, "I don't want to love. I don't want to be loved. Just leave me to myself." It is a Judgment that the unrepentant sinner will himself have made; God is there merely to ratify the truth of what it really means.[3]

As C. S. Lewis so eloquently put it,

There are only two kinds of people in the end: those who say to God, "Thy will be done," and those to whom God says, in the end, "Thy will be done." All that are in Hell, choose it. Without that self-choice there could be no Hell. No soul that seriously and constantly desires joy will ever miss it. Those who seek find. To those who knock it is opened.[4]

But what about all those passages that talk about burning in the lake of fire? Don't we have to take the idea of hell as punishment seriously? Absolutely. Hell is certainly punishment.

However, that does not mean that this punishment is not a natural consequence of rebellion against God. The key is to realize that the punishment people receive in hell is not an arbitrary pain inflicted just for the sake of inflicting pain, which is what human punishment often amounts to. It is not vindictive. I recently talked with an ex-Muslim who had rejected Islam largely because he would not accept a vision of hell in which sinners have their flesh burned off, then grown back on again, then burned off again in an eternal cycle of torture. He assumed the Christian teaching was basically the same. It isn't. Hell is not pain for the sake of pain. It is the punishment that is inherent in rejecting God. To not love God is a form of punishment in itself; indeed it is worse than what we normally think of as punishment. From Peter Kreeft:

> *What* is hell? The popular image of demons gleefully poking pitchforks into unrepentant posteriors misses the point of the biblical image of fire. Fire *destroys.* . . . Hell is not eternal life with torture but something far worse: eternal dying. . . . The images for hell in Scripture are horrible, but they're only symbols. The thing symbolized is not less horrible than the symbols, but *more.* Spiritual fire is worse than material fire; spiritual death is worse than physical death. The pain of loss—the loss of God, who is the source of all joy—is infinitely more horrible than any torture could ever be.[5]

Kreeft notes elsewhere that many believe the existence of hell dictates that God must be a God of wrath and vengeance and hate.

> But this conclusion does not follow from the premise of hell. It may be that the very love of God for the sinner constitutes the sinner's torture in hell. That love would threaten and torture the egotism that the damned sinners insist on and cling to. A

small child in a fit of rage, sulking and hating his parents, may feel their hugs and kisses at that moment as torture. By the same psychological principle, the massive beauty of an opera may be torture to someone blindly jealous of its composer. So the fires of hell may be made of the very love of God, or rather by the damned's hatred of that love.[6]

But what about judgment day? Doesn't that involve handing out particular punishments for particular sins against God? Again, it is important to understand that God's judgment is not an arbitrary list of penalties he cooked up in response to certain crimes. Judgment too should be understood as a natural consequence of our sin. God's judgment is all about the truth being revealed to all. God is not a judge in the sense that we usually think of. He doesn't weigh various arguments in court, make a decision based on his best attempt at interpreting the evidence, and then pick a punishment that he thinks best suits the crime. God doesn't weigh the merits of various competing positions on judgment day. He simply reveals the true position. Judgment day is not the day God decides the verdict on your life, it is the day when the verdict of your life is made clearly known to all. Joseph Ratzinger writes,

> In death, a human being emerges into the light of full reality and truth. He takes up that place which is truly his by right. The masquerade of living with its constant retreat behind posturings and fictions is now over. Man is what he is in truth. Judgment consists in this removal of the mask in death. The judgment is simply the manifestation of the truth.[7]

When people come face-to-face with Jesus, who is the truth, his very presence will be the final judgment. The reality of each person's relationship with him will be revealed. Either he knows us and welcomes us home or he doesn't (Matthew 7:23).

Let's address one final question before we move on from this section. It comes from a listener named Brian. Brian wasn't sold on the biblical notion of free will, so I was trying to explain to him that God desires relationship with humans; he refused to make us robots. Instead, he gave us the ability to reject him. A healthy, loving relationship is dependent on both parties being in it because they want to be, not because they have to be. I told Brian that "God understands this and so refuses to coerce us into a relationship with him. He wants us to be in it of our own accord." Brian replied,

> Didn't Jesus himself say that nonbelievers will be thrown "into the furnace of fire" where "men will weep and gnash their teeth" just as "the weeds are gathered and burned with fire" (Matthew 13:40–42 RSV)? Why then throughout the Bible is there constant appeal to transcendent punishment for nonbelievers? Transcendent punishment isn't coercion? The Old Testament seems to very much try to force man into a relationship with God. Placing a punishment on nonbelief is as close to coercion as I can ever see.

In fact, it is not coercion. To coerce (in the sense used above) is to "bring about by force or threat." To receive money or sex, say, at the point of a gun is to coerce. The threat of death brings about the action. It is important to note here that in coercion, neither death nor the action would have occurred without the coercive intrusion. In the normal course of events, a woman attacked by a rapist wouldn't have had sex with him or been shot. Only because some evil power entered her life is she forced to make a choice between two bad alternatives. That is the nature of coercion.

To accuse God of being coercive is to say, in effect, that he approaches us as completely independent beings and says, "Come with me or burn in hell." The implication is that if God would just leave us alone, we could live our lives heading toward a third alternative; one that is neither with God nor burning in hell. That is what comes to mind in Brian's phrase "placing a punishment on nonbelief." He paints a picture of a bully God arbitrarily imposing his evil desires on a peace-loving planet. Biblically, however, that is not the way the world is. Rather, the Earth is like a colony of children separated from their parents and wandering across a scorching desert. God comes to them and issues not a threat, but a warning and an offer. He says, "You are going to die out here if you do not let me help you. Please let me help you. I have plenty of water to drink and food to eat and shelter from the sand and the sun. I am your only hope of avoiding the terrible consequences of being out in this wasteland. Please, come to me." Indeed, this is almost exactly what God says in many places in Scripture.

> Come, all you who are thirsty, come to the waters;
> and you who have no money, come, buy and eat!
> Come, buy wine and milk without money and without
>   cost.
> Why spend money on what is not bread, and your labor
>   on what does not satisfy?
> Listen, listen to me, and eat what is good, and you will
>   delight in the richest of fare.
> Give ear and come to me; listen, that you may live.
>
> Isaiah 55:1–3

Come to me, all you who are weary and burdened, and I will give you rest. Take my yoke upon you and learn from me, for I am gentle and humble in heart, and you will find rest for your souls.

Matthew 11:28–29

Jerusalem, Jerusalem, you who kill the prophets and stone those sent to you, how often I have longed to gather your children together, as a hen gathers her chicks under her wings, and you were not willing.

Matthew 23:37

This is clearly not coercion. It is a statement of fact. God created us for relationship with him. In that relationship is life, joy, love, purpose, and a lot of other great things. Because healthy relationships require freedom on the part of each participant, God gave us the opportunity to opt out and forgo all those benefits. However, leaving God leads to only one place—hell. If you will not have God, you will necessarily have the opposite of that—separation from God, otherwise known as hell. There are no other alternatives, no plethora of roads to travel. It's either relationship with God or separation from him. As we will see more clearly in the next chapter, Jesus comes to show us the way home. He doesn't coerce or threaten, he simply warns and informs and beckons: "I am the way, the truth, and the life. Come with me" (see John 14:6).

We have seen in this section that the doctrine of hell is not irreconcilable with the love of God. Indeed, it is a necessary consequence of the love of God. The bigger problem, it has been said, is how to reconcile hell with human sanity.[8] Why would anyone in their right mind not choose the joy that comes with relationship with God? The sad and clearly evident truth is that sin *is* a form of insanity and that all of us sometimes deliberately refuse joy and truth. Every sin reflects that preference and shows us that the human race is "spiritually insane."[9]

Is Focusing on Heaven Detrimental to Life on Earth?

Having discussed the notion that hell cannot be reconciled with a loving God, we will conclude this chapter by briefly addressing two other common misconceptions about the Christian doctrines of heaven and hell:

The first error is that belief in life after death causes people to be less concerned with life here and now. Skeptics argue that those who are too focused on heaven become no earthly good and may even be a detriment to the planet. Living for eternity is seen as escapist and harmful.

They couldn't be more wrong. In truth, chasing hard after heaven leads to a much better life here on Earth.

The August 29, 2011 episode of Australian *X Factor* presented a good example of this fact. By most accounts that particular show was pretty standard fare until Emmanuel Kelly took the stage. The audience applauded politely as the young man with obvious limb deficiencies limped to the microphone to face the judges. Then a shocked silence fell over the crowd when Emmanuel answered Ronan Keating's question about how old he was:

"I, um, well, actually I am not exactly sure. When I was originally found in Iraq in an orphanage—my mum found me—I was found with no birth certificate, no passport, nothing. " Emmanuel, as the audience then learned via a recorded video clip, was born in a war zone and his deformities were caused by chemical weapons. He and his brother were found abandoned in a shoe box in a park and taken to an orphanage. There they were discovered by humanitarian Moira Kelly and flown to Australia for surgery. "It was like looking at an angel when Mum, Moira Kelly, walked through the orphanage door," Emmanuel reported. Moira then "fell in love" with the boys and adopted them, raising them in what certainly appeared on television to be a very loving and happy family. "My hero would have to be my mother," said Emmanuel.[10]

The video clip ended with most of the audience members and judges already on the verge of tears. Then they were pushed completely over the edge when Emmanuel began to sing. His song choice for the event: John Lennon's "Imagine." You are probably familiar with the lyrics. Lennon asks his listeners to envision a reality in which heaven, hell, and religion don't exist. In such a state, he believes wars would cease and everyone would live together in harmony.

If the studio audience and over 14 million views on YouTube are any indication, it was a very moving performance. Personally, I found it mostly ironic. As much as I enjoyed Emmanuel's singing, the ridiculous juxtaposition of a boy who had been rescued by nuns of Mother Teresa's Missionaries of Charity and then adopted and raised by the founder of the Children's First Foundation, a woman whose "Catholic faith has been her driving force to [help children in need] in New York's Bronx, Calcutta, the Kalahari, Western Australia and all around the world,"[11] singing about how belief in heaven and hell is the cause of great pain and suffering was simply too much for me. I don't know if Emmanuel actually believes that getting rid of religion and the Christian doctrines regarding the afterlife would be beneficial to the world, but I know that his own life is evidence that points in exactly the opposite direction. Emmanuel received the abundant blessings in his life precisely because some people were convinced of the reality of heaven and hell. Christianity hasn't caused him to suffer; it has lifted him up.

Unfortunately, Lennon's thesis is quite widely accepted among skeptics, so it is important to recognize it and be able to correct this false view. They charge that people who seek after heaven and try to avoid hell are too focused on the afterlife to bother making this world a better place. This is simply not the case. Biblical religion is not opposed to the betterment of the world. Indeed, Christianity has been the premier means by which the conditions of this planet have become better, a point very ably argued by such thinkers as Thomas Woods (*How the Catholic*

Church Built Western Civilization), Rodney Stark (*The Victory of Reason*), and Vishal Mangalwadi (*The Book that Made Your World*). C. S. Lewis adds:

> If you read history, you will find that the Christians who did most for the present world were just those who thought the most of the next. The Apostles themselves, who set on foot the conversion of the Roman Empire, the great men who built up the Middle Ages, the English Evangelicals who abolished the Slave Trade, all left their mark on Earth, precisely because their minds were occupied with Heaven. It is since Christians have largely ceased to think of the other world that they have become so ineffective in this. Aim at heaven and you will get earth "thrown in": aim at earth and you will get neither.[12]

One of the major reasons for this fact is biblical religion's distinctive eschatological view of time. Most worldviews view time pessimistically. Eastern religions (and Western paganism) view history as either a vicious cycle or a march away from an idyllic moment in the past. Thus, the goal of these worldviews is to escape the cycle and the degradation. Western materialism's view is that time is ultimately meaningless, a position elucidated beautifully by Shakespeare's *Macbeth*:

> To-morrow, and to-morrow, and to-morrow,
> Creeps in this petty pace from day to day,
> To the last syllable of recorded time;
> And all our yesterdays have lighted fools
> The way to dusty death. Out, out, brief candle!
> Life's but a walking shadow, a poor player,
> That struts and frets his hour upon the stage,
> And then is heard no more. It is a tale
> Told by an idiot, full of sound and fury,
> Signifying nothing.[13]

116

For biblical religion, however, time is charged with meaning in that God is actively working to redeem all of creation. Those with a Christian worldview are looking forward to the new creation as the culmination and fulfillment of God's ongoing work. Christians don't look to escape time or return to the garden of Eden; instead, like Abraham, they are looking forward to the "city with foundations, whose architect and builder is God" (Hebrews 11:10).

In chapter 6 we saw the basic framework of God's redemptive plan. It involves a pattern that is readily apparent throughout history. G. K. Beale rightly summarizes it this way: "(1) cosmic chaos followed by (2) new creation, (3) commission of kingship for divine glory, (4) sinful fall, and (5) exile"[14] at which time God starts another new creation. In each instance of the pattern, God creates a family, under the headship of one man, with a mandate to be fruitful and take care of the Earth. Then this family rebels against God and ends up in exile from him. God then re-creates the family and the pattern starts again.

Let's review this pattern briefly. Adam and Eve were the first family, but they rebelled and got kicked out of the garden. God started again with Noah and his family, but they rebelled as well and were scattered throughout the Earth after the Tower of Babel. The pattern repeated with Moses and the Israelites. They rebelled at Kadesh Barnea and had to wander in the wilderness for forty years, exiled from the Promised Land. Then the Israelites went through a new creation event and a smaller "Red Sea" as they crossed the Jordan River to conquer the land, and King David, as the next new Adam, established the family as a kingdom of God on earth. However, rebellion ensued once more, and the family was exiled by the Syrians and Babylonians. Jesus, as the final new Adam, gave birth to the final new family and established the final new kingdom. Notice that each stage in this pattern of creation involves looking ahead and working toward the fulfillment of the pattern, the final new creation. Christians view the time in which we currently live as the last stage (the "last days," to use New Testament terminology) before that blessed event. Consequently, we actively work, just as God's children have always worked, to fulfill the mandate God has given us. The practical result of this eschatological view of time is not that Christians sit around and wait for the New Jerusalem to arrive. Rather, we actively work to see it accomplished.

Peter Kreeft writes,

> People think that heaven is escapist because they fear that thinking about heaven will distract us from living well here and now. It is exactly the opposite, and the lives of the saints and our Lord himself prove it. Those who truly love heaven will do the most for earth. It's easy to see why. Those who love the homeland best work the hardest in the colonies to make them resemble the homeland. "Thy kingdom come . . . on earth as it is in heaven."[15]

Is Heaven Going to Be Boring?

L.A. *Times* columnist Joel Stein raised a few hackles in 2007 when Starbucks printed one of his quotes on their venti cups:

> Heaven is totally overrated. It seems boring. Clouds, listening to people play the harp. It should be somewhere you can't wait to go, like a luxury hotel. Maybe blue skies and soft music were enough to keep people in line in the seventeenth century, but heaven has to step it up a bit. They're basically getting by because they only have to be better than hell.

It is an old joke, as Stein himself later realized. In a piece about the controversy the cup had created, he noted: "Gary Larson did it in a 'Far Side' cartoon with a guy on a cloud saying, 'Wish I'd brought a magazine.' Mark Twain did it in *Huckleberry Finn*.

Isaac Asimov—who was not even funny—said, 'For whatever the tortures of hell, I think the boredom of heaven would be even worse.'"[16]

I don't think so. And actually, this is a far more serious subject than it might seem at first glance. Stein may have made his point in a lighthearted way, but he was obviously touching on a serious objection to heaven, one that I hear quite often. As Kreeft notes, "No one can run with hope or passion toward a goal that seems boring."[17] Therefore, we must be able to recognize and counter the bad theology that is present here and present a vision of heaven that is more biblically accurate and attractive.

That may well start with reading some of Randy Alcorn's work. In response to Stein's coffee cup quote, at least five people sent him a copy of Alcorn's book *Heaven,* and I recommend it as well. Alcorn offers a wide-ranging biblical look at what heaven will be like and does a great job of debunking the notion that it will be an ethereal place with not much to do. His major point is that it will be a new Earth, where real people with real bodies will be "eating, drinking, working, playing, traveling, worshiping, and discovering."[18] I will entrust you to Alcorn with this general topic, except to make one brief point about eternity and how we experience time.

Objections to heaven and hell often center on the fact that they are supposed to last forever. Even if one grants that there will be lots to do in heaven, it seems inconceivable that we will want to do these things forever. And as for hell, even if one accepts that people choose to go there and deserve to go there, it doesn't seem fair that people should have to go there forever.

One key to addressing this issue is to recognize that our experience of time doesn't have much to do with how many actual objective units of time have passed. It has much more to do with the quality of the experience we are having. We simply don't experience every passing moment the same way. Some seem longer and some don't seem to have any length at all. In other words, there isn't much of a correspondence between how many objective units of time have passed and how much time we feel has passed. The difference in our experience of time usually depends on whether or not we are enjoying what we are doing and whether or not we find it important.

For example, sometimes it feels like time passes very quickly. Think about that first date with your special someone. You started talking and before you knew it four hours had gone by. But it felt like only a few minutes. On the other hand, now think about the most boring lecture you ever had to sit through. The clock just seemed to stop, right?

So in one instance the time seemed to pass very quickly, and in the other, it just dragged along. Each minute of the date was like a split second, but each minute of the lecture was like an hour. Moments are light and fleeting in the date, but heavy and slow in the lecture.

Now, think about these events after they are finished. Something very interesting happens. Those moments that seemed so small and fleeting while we were on the date are the ones that now become large and heavy in our minds. Each second is solid and almost visible; you can remember how the evening played out step by step. You can almost smell the food and hear his or her voice; you can enjoy taking in all the details again and again because they are right there for you all the time. The event has a continual reality; there is a sense in which it has become eternal.

On the other hand, that lecture is now like it never even happened. You can't remember one thing that was said and frankly, that doesn't bother you because you never gave that class another thought. It's like a wisp, something you can't really grasp even if you wanted to (and you don't). The event that seemed so solid and heavy as you experienced it is now nothing; it has no weight, no substance.

I think our experience of time in this life gives us some insight into heaven and hell. To focus on how many moments we will exist in either place is to miss the point. The number of moments won't matter in heaven and hell; what will matter is our experience. In heaven our experience will be of such a high quality that we'll never think about time passing because we will be enjoying ourselves too much. And this experience won't be fleeting; it will have weight and importance. All of our moments will have the solidity of eternity.

On the other hand, the experience of hell will be of such a low quality that, again, the number of moments won't actually matter because each moment will seem to take forever. On top of that, these moments won't have any solidity to them. A person in hell won't be able to grab on to anything. Life will be wispy, unreal.

So heaven and hell will both be eternal, but that has little to do with how long anyone will be in either state of existence.

Conclusion

Regis Martin writes that all the choices of our life "carry us to one or another everlasting end": heaven or hell.

> Surely no two words summon more powerfully the latent and dramatic possibilities of being human. The image of the one conjuring all that is most deeply embedded in human desire and longing: joy, freedom, peace, delight, perfection, God. The other an image of sorrows unspeakable, compacted of all that we most dread and abhor: infernal solitude, enmity, evil, ennui.[19]

This is the truth we must try to convey to those who question Christian beliefs about the afterlife.

How to Think About the Bible

The Bible as a Fax From Heaven

In one of the more famous passages from Dan Brown's mega best seller *The Da Vinci Code*, the primary antagonist of the book, Sir Leigh Teabing, boldly claims to sum up "everything you need to know about the Bible" by suggesting that it is not a divine book: "The Bible did not arrive by fax from heaven. . . . [It] is a product of *man*. . . . Not of God. The Bible did not fall magically from the clouds. Man created it as a historical record of tumultuous times."[1]

In the novel this speech is intended to be a strong attack on Christianity, something that will shake a believer's faith to the core. This is interesting because most of the speech is made up of statements that Christians should agree with. After all, it's true that the Bible did not arrive by fax from heaven or fall magically from the clouds. It is also a fact that the Bible is a product of humans and a historic record of tumultuous times. So why did Teabing think it was such a revolutionary and important announcement? The key is the three words in the middle of his statement. Teabing thinks that if the Bible is a product of humans, it cannot be from God.

His argument goes something like this: Either the Bible came from God or it came from humans. If it came from God it would have arrived all at once as a complete package in some supernatural way. But we know from studying history that the canon developed over time and was written in the same way as every other document, by humans. Therefore, it is not from God.

In other words, he seems to think that if the Bible is not a magic book written by the very fingers of God, then it should not be accepted as divine or authoritative. This simply does not follow. The problem with the argument is that it presents a false dichotomy as the first premise, and the second premise is simply false. The Bible can be authored by both God and humans, and there is no reason to think that if God is going to provide us with a document that it must arrive all at once.

As we will see in this chapter, Teabing's reasoning is based on a misunderstanding of what the Bible claims to be and how it fits within the scope and nature of divine revelation. Unfortunately, this bad theology and faulty logic are very common among skeptics and play a major role in keeping them from Christianity. Teabing may be a fictional character, but the ideas Dan Brown gave him to espouse are a very real stumbling block to many actual unbelievers.

The Biblicist View of Scripture

The theological error we will be addressing in this chapter goes by many names, but we will refer to it as biblicism. Here is a summary of the main ideas of this view as understood by the average skeptic:

The Bible is the Word of God. By that I mean that Scripture consists of written propositions literally spoken from on high. Because it is from God, each syllable should be read as if it was dictated by the very lips of the Almighty or written by his fingers as a declaration to mankind. Therefore, we are not to interpret Scripture as we would any regular human book. We don't have to look at historical context or try to discern what genre of human literature is being used. God is outside of our earthly limitations, so we must interpret his words in a very literal way. Indeed, some would say that we shouldn't try to interpret the Bible at all; we should just read it and accept what it says. In the words of the bumper sticker, GOD SAID IT. I BELIEVE IT. THAT SETTLES IT.

New Testament scholar Russell Pregeant tells about a student with this view:

> The young woman—a student in my undergraduate course in New Testament—was adamant. She insisted that her particular religious group was not burdened by human doctrines; the members of this group relied solely upon the Bible for their beliefs. There was no sense arguing about what the Bible means in any particular instance, because it means what it says and says what it means. And, of course, this group thought of its beliefs as the absolute truth, since they were based not upon fallible human interpretation but directly upon the Bible itself.[2]

"But Snails Don't Melt and Snakes Don't Eat Dirt"

Unfortunately, many skeptics assume that the student's approach to Scripture is the "Christian" approach, so they latch on to it and use it as a weapon to then debunk the Bible. They start by interpreting the text very literally, pick out a few passages that can't possibly be true if understood that way, and then assume they have shown that Scripture is unreliable. This can actually get rather humorous at times.

For example, the popular skeptic website infidels.org offers a list of biblical contradictions that include the following gems:

- The fact that snails do not melt. This is presented as a rebuttal of the King James Version of Psalm 58:8: "As a snail which melteth, let every one of them pass away: like the untimely birth of a woman, that they may not see the sun."
- The fact that "snakes, while built low, do not eat dirt." Consequently, according to the list's author, Jim Merritt, we know that Genesis 3:14 is completely bogus because it states: "And the Lord God said unto the serpent, Because thou hast done this, thou art cursed above all cattle, and above every beast of the field; upon thy belly shalt thou go, and dust shalt thou eat all the days of thy life" (KJV).
- The fact that the earth is shaped like a ball. This supposedly lays waste to the claims of Isaiah 40:22 (KJV): "It is he that sitteth upon the circle of the earth, and the inhabitants thereof are as grasshoppers; that stretcheth out the heavens as a curtain, and spreadeth them out as a tent to dwell in" and Matthew 4:8 (KJV): "Again, the devil taketh him up into an exceeding high mountain, and sheweth him all the kingdoms of the world, and the glory of them." Merritt notes that "astronomical bodies are spherical, and you cannot see the entire exterior surface from anyplace. The kingdoms of Egypt, China, Greece, Crete, sections of Asia Minor, India, Maya (in Mexico), Carthage (North Africa), Rome (Italy), Korea, and other settlements from these kingdoms of the world were widely distributed."[3]

I guess that settles it then. To the obvious response that the authors of these biblical texts are using metaphorical and poetic language, Merritt scoffs that this is not an option for those who want to treat the Bible as the "absolute WORD OF GOD."[4]

According to Merritt, if you are going to treat the Bible as divine, you have to read all the language very literally. If a passage only makes sense if it is interpreted metaphorically, Merritt thinks that this shows that the Bible is not directly from God. After all, you shouldn't "interpret" Scripture; you should just "read" it.

He thinks that God's Word, by its nature, could not allow for the use of normal human language. So he is under the impression that we cannot read and interpret the Bible the same way we would read and interpret any other book. He treats it as a magic tome written with a "divine literalism" and then thinks he has debunked that idea by showing that not all of its claims can be literally true because they contradict scientific facts about the world. These are commonly referred to as "external biblical contradictions."

"But Jesus Called People Names"

Skeptics also use this method to point out supposed contradictions within the text itself. These "internal contradictions" seem to be of almost endless supply, but in general they all have one thing in common: a refusal to read the Bible with anything but a harsh literalism. For example, in his book *Losing Faith in Faith: From Preacher to Atheist,* Dan Barker devotes a chapter to "Bible Contradictions." He writes, "Why do trained theologians differ? Why do educated translators disagree over Greek and Hebrew meanings? Why all the confusion? Shouldn't a document that was 'divinely inspired' by an omniscient and omnipotent deity be as clear as possible?"[5] He then offers a list of supposed discrepancies, including:

Was Jesus peaceable?

John 14:27 KJV: "Peace I leave with you, my peace I give unto you."

Acts 10:36 KJV: "The word which God sent unto the children of Israel, preaching peace by Jesus Christ . . ."

Luke 2:14 KJV: ". . . on earth peace, good will toward men."

versus:

Matthew 10:34–36 KJV: "Think not that I am come to send peace on earth: I came not to send peace, but a sword. For I am come to set a man at variance against his father, and the daughter against her mother, and the daughter in law against her mother in law. And a man's foes shall be they of his own household."

Luke 22:36 KJV: "Then said he unto them . . . he that hath no sword, let him sell his garment, and buy one."

Shall we call people names?

Matthew 5:22 KJV: "Whosoever shall say, Thou fool, shall be in danger of hell fire." [Jesus speaking]

versus:

Matthew 23:17 KJV: "Ye fools and blind . . ." [Jesus speaking]

Psalm 14:1 KJV: "The fool hath said in his heart, There is no God."[6]

Again, I trust that you can see that these are fairly easy passages to deal with if you are willing to allow for normal rules of interpretation (some details of which we will discuss below). Jesus' teaching in the Sermon on the Mount that we should not treat people with contempt clearly does not contradict his statement in Matthew 23 about the objective intellectual and moral standing of hypocritical religious leaders who teach lies, for example. However, Barker assumes and then debunks a Biblicist view of Scripture that would not allow for such a reading.

In this chapter we will see how all of the above objections are based on a false understanding of the nature of God's revelation and an improper view of where the Bible fits into it. Skeptics tend to react against the Biblicist view that revelation *is* the Bible. They envision God's revelation as a systematic theology textbook being dropped out of the sky and think that this is supposed to be all that God has ever done or will do in the way of communication and disclosure.

However, as we study the sources and the substance of revelation, we will see that this is too narrow a view. These skeptics are reacting, once again, to bad theology.

General Revelation

Biblicists (and the skeptics who try to debunk them) tend to treat Scripture as the only source of revelation. However, Scripture itself teaches that is not the case:

> The heavens declare the glory of God;
> the skies proclaim the work of his hands.
> Day after day they pour forth speech;
> night after night they reveal knowledge.
> They have no speech, they use no words;
> no sound is heard from them.
> Yet their voice goes out into all the earth,
> their words to the ends of the world.
> Psalm 19:1–4

The wrath of God is being revealed from heaven against all the godlessness and wickedness of people, who suppress the truth by their wickedness, since what may be known about God is plain to them, because God has made it plain to them. For since the creation of the world God's invisible qualities—his eternal power and divine nature—have been clearly seen, being understood from what has been made, so that men are without excuse.

Romans 1:18–20

According to these passages, people receive some revelation of God simply by living in the world he created. This knowledge of God is available to everyone through creation and our ability to reason. This is usually referred to as "general" or "universal" revelation. As Roger Olson notes, "With the possible exception of [Karl] Barth and a few other modern neoorthodox theologians, the vast majority of Christians have always believed that God is revealed, however vaguely, in the natural order he created, including human existence itself."[7]

Special Revelation: Words and Deeds

A second type of revelation is called special or particular revelation. It is the action of God in a specific time and place in history to reveal something that people otherwise would not have known through natural revelation. The Biblicist view is that special revelation occurs at that time and place where God speaks from heaven, and those words get written down. Accordingly, the words themselves are the extent of revelation and we have those words in the Bible. However, in actuality special revelation is much broader than that. It is not limited only to the words of the Bible; it involves both those words *and* the events to which those words point.

In revealing himself, God doesn't hand down a document or merely offer a statement for his prophet to write down. He also acts. From the very beginning of the world, God has been an active participant in history, revealing through both word and deed. From creation to the flood (long before we had any kind of Bible), to the Exodus to the conquest of Canaan, to the birth and ministry of Jesus and beyond, God has not only spoken to and through prophets, but personally directed history and performed signs and wonders to accompany his proclamations.

There are at least two reasons for this.

The first is that both words and deeds are necessary for a full understanding of God. Actions help us understand the words, and words help us make sense of the actions.

For example, as Vishal Mangalwadi notes, even when God gave the Ten Commandments (about as close to a fax from heaven as we get in history), God introduced the first command by saying, "I am the LORD your God, who brought you out of Egypt, out of the land of slavery" (Exodus 20:2–3). The context of the giving of the Ten Commandments is the exodus from Egypt. The Hebrews had just been through several extraordinary experiences with God. He had sent plagues, parted the Red Sea, fed them with manna, and given them water from a rock, among many other signs and wonders. These acts are all part of God's revelation. Before God spoke words from the mountain, he had already been making himself known to the Jews through his works. The propositions he gave Moses from on high were part of that revelation, but just a part. They helped clarify something about the God that the Hebrews already knew from his acts. The words and the works went together to provide a fuller revelation, one that would not have been possible if God had only spoken.

> They knew *Who* their deliverer was through His wonderful works in their history and His power over physical nature. God communicated in words because His works in nature and culture cannot always be understood unless He also explains them. Nor can His word be understood unless we also examine His works.[8]

Mangalwadi also points out that Jesus "used this same Old Testament epistemology: He asked skeptics to believe His words because of empirically observable works that demonstrated who He was (John 5:35–37; 10:25, 37–38; 14:11–12)."[9] The gospel of John is intensely theological; it contains some very deep propositional teaching about who Jesus is. In that sense it is revelation that consists of words. However, John structured his gospel around seven major miracles of Jesus and explained:

> Jesus did many other miraculous signs in the presence of his disciples, which are not recorded in this book. But these are written that you may believe that Jesus is the Christ, the Son of God, and that by believing you may have life in his name.
>
> John 20:30–31 NIV1984

John realized that the words and deeds go together. Jesus' miracles helped explain and verify his teaching.

This is how all human communication functions: Words and works explain and confirm each other. *Dei Verbum* 2 sums up this point nicely:

> The plan of revelation is realized by deeds and words having an inner unity: the deeds wrought by God in the history of salvation manifest and confirm the teachings and realities signified by the words while the words proclaim the deeds and clarify the mystery contained in them.[10]

The second reason God uses both words and works is that God does not just offer us propositions about himself—he offers us himself. The goal of revelation is personal relationship. God doesn't only want us to know about him as a third grader might know about an ancient ruler of Rome, God wants us to know him as children know their parents or wives know their husbands.

Intimate personal relationships are not built only through an exchange of truth claims. Sending faxes back and forth might help you learn *about* someone, but it wouldn't actually allow you to get to *know* them. Rather, people get to know each other by spending time together; they share experiences. That is exactly what God wants to do with us. He wants to know and be known in a very personal way.

As such, since the beginning of time, God has made himself known by actually interacting with humans on earth. He has revealed himself by breaking into time and space to share experiences with us. God hasn't just spoken to people from the clouds (although that has happened occasionally) or simply given them words to read (although he has done that too), but he has revealed himself through the events of history. "Through divine revelation, God chose to show forth and communicate Himself and the eternal decisions of His will regarding the salvation of men."[11] God doesn't just communicate his thoughts and commands, he communicates himself.

God's revelation of himself finds its clearest expression, of course, in the person of Jesus Christ. "If there is any one belief that unites all Christians it is that Jesus Christ is God's unique and unsurpassable self-disclosure."[12] The event in time and space that all of God's other acts in history pointed toward is the incarnation.

> God, after He spoke long ago to the fathers in the prophets in many portions and in many ways, in these last days has spoken to us in His Son, whom He appointed heir of all things, through whom also He made the world.
>
> Hebrews 1:1–2 NASB

God's ultimate act in history was to actually be born as a human baby in a small corner of the Roman Empire about 2,000 years ago. If we want to know God and learn what he has to say to us, it is to the carpenter from Galilee that we need to look. In Jesus, God gave himself to us in the fullest sense of the term. Jesus was not only a great prophet or teacher. He did not just offer principles for us to follow or ideals to aspire to, as if the content of what he said was the revelation. Jesus himself was the revelation. Jesus didn't say, "Here is the truth, follow it." He said, "I am the truth, follow me" (see John 14:6).

Revelation, the Bible, and Jesus

So if revelation comes to us through creation in general as well as the specific acts and words of God in history, where does the Bible fit in? Clearly it is an aspect of special revelation, but in what way? If it isn't a fax from heaven, what is it? What should we say to the skeptics who are misusing Scripture?

I would suggest that you first try to make clear that God's revelation is not limited to the text of the Bible. It also includes the events and the person to which the words point. In other words, we should not treat the Bible as if the book itself is the end all and be all of God's revelation. It is a means to a greater end. The Bible is a tool we can use to get to God's full revelation. We should not strive to know the Bible for its own sake; we should strive to know the Bible as a means to knowing God. More specifically, we should use the Bible to get to know Jesus.

C. S. Lewis wrote in a letter to a friend that "It is Christ Himself, not the Bible, who is the true Word of God. The Bible, read in the right spirit and with the guidance of good teachers will bring us to Him."[13] Lewis's point here is not that the Bible is not divine, but that it is not the fullness of God's revelation. That distinction belongs to Jesus. In regard to the term *Word of God,* I believe Lewis would agree with *Dei Verbum* 24: "The

Sacred Scriptures contain the Word of God and since they are inspired really are the word of God."[14] Lewis understood that the function of Scripture is to convey a reality that goes beyond the language of the text. Getting at that reality is the important thing. The words of Scripture are the vessels carrying the treasure of God's Word. As Michael Christensen rightly implores, "Let us not mistake the vessels for the treasure nor fail to find the treasure in the vessels."[15]

Indeed, making that mistake can actually keep people from the intimate relationship God wants with us through Christ. A Biblicist is prone to view God as if he were a distant father who sent letters to his children long ago. As John Webster noted: "Accounts of scriptural inspiration are not infrequently curiously *deistic*, insofar as the biblical text can itself become a revelatory agent by virtue of an act of divine inspiration *in the past*."[16] However, in reality, God is a dad who wants to live with his children and take part in their daily lives *right now*. Biblicism keeps God farther away from us than he wants to be.

We must not substitute knowing the Bible for knowing Jesus. Realizing that the Bible is a tool that God uses for revelation rather than the fullness of revelation is a good place to start. We don't want to be like the religious leaders whom Jesus scolded for rejecting him while claiming to remain faithful to Scripture: "You study the Scriptures diligently because you think that in them you have eternal life. These are the very Scriptures that testify about me, yet you refuse to come to me to have life" (John 5:39–40).

How to Interpret and Understand the Bible

So if the Bible is not to be read with a radical literalism, as if it were a magic fax, how should we read it? How can we use

Scripture as a means to closer relationship with God? In this section we will look at a framework for biblical interpretation and offer some principles for discovering all that God has for us in the Bible. We will see that in a certain respect the Bible must be approached in the same way as any other piece of literature. However, there is obviously much more to it than that, as Scripture is uniquely inspired of God. I will argue that we should read the Bible the way the church fathers did. This involves looking for the literal sense of Scripture as well as a spiritual sense.

The literal sense of the text is primarily the meaning intended by the author. (Note that finding the literal sense is not the same as interpreting every word literally. We have already established that we should not do that. Every written work in the world has a literal sense, but not every work should be interpreted literally.) To find the literal sense, one uses the tools of textual and historical analysis to discover information, such as the author, the audience, the genre of the work, and the cultural situation at the time of the writing. The goal in finding the literal sense is to get as accurate a picture as possible of what God was doing when he broke into time and space in the past. We want to try to get into the author's shoes as much as possible so that we can understand the nature of God's revelation as it was experienced and understood at the time he revealed it. If God reveals himself through words and events, we want to understand the context of both as clearly as possible in order to receive the full revelation.

The spiritual sense of Scripture is a broader meaning that God wanted to convey that may not have been intended or known to the original author or audience. Finding the spiritual sense involves connecting one or more of God's revelatory acts to one or more of his other acts. It is about seeing how all of God's actions in history fit together to reveal God's character and his plan for the world. Let's take a quick look at each of the senses of Scripture in more detail.

Finding the Literal Sense of Scripture

We have seen that "the Bible, in effect, does not present itself as a direct revelation of timeless truths but as the written testimony to a series of interventions in which God reveals himself in human history."[17] In other words, the Bible is not a systematic theology or science or philosophy textbook full of propositions dictated by a God who is outside of time and culture. Rather, it is a record of God's revelation in history as recorded by humans. It is very much inside of time and culture.

As such, revelation has a very human element. Revelation is divine but it is not completely otherworldly. It is down-to-earth in many senses of the term. A major flaw of the Biblicist approach to the Bible is its failure to accept the human dimension of Scripture.

There is an interesting example of this in Sam Harris's *Letter to a Christian Nation*. Harris takes a shot at the Bible by suggesting that if it really was written by an omniscient deity surely . . .

> it would make perfectly accurate predictions about human events. You would expect it to contain a passage such as "In the latter half of the twentieth century, humankind will develop a globally linked system of computers—the principles of which I set forth in Leviticus—and this system shall be called the Internet." The Bible contains nothing like this. In fact, it does not contain a single sentence that could not have been written by a man or woman living in the first century. This should trouble you.[18]

If the Bible is a revelation of God, Harris assumes, it would not be limited to what people knew in the first century. It would include a few facts they didn't have access to yet. Harris thinks the Bible should have fallen down from heaven complete with information about DNA and instructions on how to cure cancer.[19] The fact that it was obviously written by human hands with human language within the context of an ancient culture is proof to Harris that it was not written by the finger of God. This is a fundamentalist understanding of revelation.

Because Biblicists don't accept the human element of revelation, they tend to try to interpret the Bible without accounting for the cultural context of the writing. In other words, they don't look for the literal sense of Scripture.

The reason for that is quite simple: If the Bible is a magic fax from heaven, there is no need to study the cultural context into which it came. However, it is not a fax from heaven. God does not reveal himself to us independent of human culture or the conditions of language. God is incarnational. He comes to us where we are; he lives with us and speaks our language. Therefore, we have to understand the culture and the language into which God reveals. We cannot impose our own culture and language (or views of what God should be like) onto the text. Rather, interpretation of biblical revelation should start by using the same principles of historical and textual analysis that we use to understand any ancient human literature: First we find the literal sense of the text.

For example, Peter Kreeft and Ronald Tacelli point out that we should try to "read the book in the same spirit or mind as its author wrote it" rather than "try to understand the author's mind through the colored eyeglasses of your own worldview, assumptions, beliefs, categories, ideologies or prejudices."[20]

Also, we should interpret a book according to its genre. One should not interpret poetry, law, parable, biography, science, religion, myth, and history in exactly the same way. Discovering the genre of a particular book of the Bible is essential. We have to be able to separate moral fables like Jesus' parables from eyewitness description like the miracles in the Gospels.

Reading With an "Open Heart" Is Not Enough

To find the literal sense of Scripture, then, we need to use the normal tools of literary criticism.[21] By refusing to submit Scripture to this scholarship, Biblicists separate themselves from the fullness of God's revelation. Sadly, they also keep skeptics from that revelation as well, and in the process encourage unbelievers to reject God and the Bible based on a false view of revelation.

A sad example of this can be found at losingmyreligion.com, a website run by former fundamentalist Christians who are now atheists. The main thrust of their work is to debunk a very literalist interpretation of Scripture. One of the more interesting sections of the site is an FAQ page where the hosts answer some of the more common questions and comments they receive, including this reasonable statement from a believer: "You are quoting Bible verses out of context. If you understood the times and the history surrounding the circumstances, you'd see it very differently." They reply:

> True. We are not Bible scholars, and do not pretend to understand the historical, cultural and linguistic background behind ancient texts. In addition, we are looking at ancient documents through multiple filters spanning time, culture, language, and our own biases, so hold no illusions that we (or the opposition) understand the Bible as it was originally penned.[22]

Unfortunately this doesn't bother these skeptics because, they say, they are simply following the example of Christians:

Untrained Christian practitioners abound. . . . Their narrow, literalist view of the Bible, and the weird morality it creates, are what most of us understand Christianity to be. These Christians take their English-translated Bibles at face value, and draw moral and ethical conclusions straight from what they selectively read. In this arena, we are as qualified as they.[23]

While that statement might be entirely correct, all it means is that nobody in this scenario is reading the Bible properly and so nobody is interacting with the Truth they should be finding through the text. Indeed, it seems that these skeptics don't actually care about truth. That suspicion is confirmed with another question: "So why don't you study Bible history, understand 'true' Christianity, and become Christians?" They answer:

First, we challenge evangelical Christians to do the same. Those who maintain that the Bible on their shelf is the literally true, inerrant word of God, have much to consider. An encounter with the sheer magnitude of the academic study of ancient texts is an eye-opening experience, one that we highly recommend to all Christians.

Second, we don't believe that God can only be found through scholarship. Certainly that would exclude most of humanity, were it a requirement. Rather we feel that an honest read of the Scripture, with prayer and an open heart, and a genuine desire to seek God, should be sufficient.

We have done this for a combined total of over 22 years, without finding anything real. If the Christian God cannot be found this way, then he is either hiding, or he is not real.[24]

And there you have another very real and dangerous result of a Biblicist understanding of revelation and the Bible. These skeptics have tried the Biblicist approach to finding God and it hasn't worked for them. They say that they would like to find God, but, following the Biblicist model, have confined themselves to search for him in only very limited ways. These guys claim they are giving the Bible an "honest read," but they are defining "honest" in a blatantly anti-intellectual way that renders finding the literal sense of the text unnecessary. They simply don't care what the human author actually meant. They think we should be able to find God through Scripture apart from scholarship (a thoroughly Biblicist position), meaning we should be able to use the Bible to find God without looking for the true literal sense of the text. However, because of the nature of God's revelation, that doesn't work. It's like saying I should be able to get to the moon on the wings of my paper airplane and then complaining when it doesn't work, "But I sincerely think that it should!"

We saw this same mind-set in the Bible student mentioned earlier who didn't think she should try to interpret the text. Of course, this is ridiculous. It is impossible to read a book without interpreting the words.[25] Olson rightly says that "Scripture is never uninterpreted except when being quoted and even then, unless the quotation is from the Hebrew, Aramaic or Greek, the translation reflects some element of interpretation."[26] As Pregeant goes on to point out:

> It is nonsensical to talk about understanding any sort of communication without interpreting it. It might seem that at least some sentences are so straightforward that their meanings are self-evident, so that no interpretation is needed. But is this really so? The fact is that not only the simplest statements but even individual words need interpretation.
>
> To understand any sort of communication, we have to interpret it, which means using our imagination to construe it in some particular way. And when we come to complex writings such as the Bible, the need for interpretation becomes even more evident. For example, in Mark 3:27, Jesus makes this startling statement: "But no one can enter a strong man's house and plunder his

property without first tying up the strong man; then indeed the house can be plundered." By itself this statement sounds like advice on burglary. But a quick glance at the context suggests that we should understand it metaphorically.[27]

If we are going to receive revelation through the Bible, we simply have to be able to recognize that metaphor. That requires scholarship. Does that mean we all have to be PhDs to know God? Of course not. However, we need to acknowledge that scriptural exegesis is a necessity. Scholarship is simply the way we access written information. From a first grader learning his ABCs to a NASA hopeful studying aeronautical engineering, getting at truth through books requires interpretation, and that is scholarship. If you want to get at the truth contained in Scripture, you need to start by finding the literal sense.

The Spiritual Sense of Scripture

Every book has that literal sense, the meaning that was intended by the human author. However, as inspired literature, the Bible also contains something unique to itself: a spiritual sense. This is the meaning that God intended for us but that may not have been known by the author or the original audience. It is found by examining the connection between historical revelations of God on three different levels: the analogical, moral, and anagogical.

The analogical sense is the meaning of a text that reveals Jesus. I have used this method of scriptural interpretation throughout this book, particularly in showing how people and events in the Old Testament are fulfilled in Christ. For example, we have seen how Adam, Noah, and Moses tell us something about the nature and ministry of Jesus.

The moral sense of Scripture reveals how one should live today. We can look to the Bible for insight about holy living and

142

the nature of church life. We are to imitate the great heroes of the faith in their courage and perseverance, for instance, and, as we saw in chapter 6, understand baptism in relation to the flood and the crossing of the Red Sea.

While the analogical sense looks back to Jesus, and the moral sense looks to the here and now, the anagogical sense looks to the future. Here we interpret texts in a way that tells us something about the glory that is to come.[28] Life in the church age prefigures certain aspects of heaven, and the New Jerusalem has been prefigured throughout history by both the original Jerusalem and the church.

When we read the Bible in the spiritual sense, we are simply doing what the New Testament writers did themselves. They constantly saw types of Jesus in the Old Testament and viewed their own time, the church age, as foreshadowing the age to come.

The Spiritual Sense and the Economy of God

I want to make just two quick points about finding the spiritual sense of Scripture.

First, the spiritual sense is always built on the literal sense of Scripture. Step one of interpreting within the fourfold sense of Scripture should always be to find out what the text was intended to mean by its author.

I've always been frustrated by the small-group Bible study model in which the leader starts by going around the circle and asking each participant, "What does this text mean to you?" That is a ridiculous place to start. The first question we should be asking is "What does this text mean to the author?" After that we can move on to other questions, such as "Do we see parallels between this passage and any others?" "What is the broader meaning of the revelatory event recorded by this text?" "What aspect of God do we see revealed here?" and "Does this aspect of God apply to a particular part of your life?" Before you can get answers to those follow-up questions, however, you have to know what the text meant at the time it was written. To not take the first step is to throw oneself into an abyss of subjectivity. You might end up with ten different interpretations that are all contradictory. Would each person be right? Of course not. To avoid this, all "spiritual" interpretations must be consistent with the literal sense. The original writer may not have realized all the levels of meanings embedded in the revelation he recorded, but those meanings cannot contradict the original.

Second, and closely related, proper spiritual interpretation must be based on the fact that God reveals himself in historical events, not just in words. Because all those historical events reveal the same God, they relate to each other as a unity. By examining the events themselves (not just the words that point to the event), we can get to know God's character and his overall plan.

We have already talked about how we get to know people better by spending time with them rather than just exchanging letters. One of the reasons for this is that we can see how they act in different circumstances. As we share a greater variety of experiences, a clear pattern will likely emerge as to the person's character and motives, among other traits. It is the same with God. As we examine his actions in history, we can compare them and detect a clear pattern as to his nature and plan. Finding the spiritual sense of Scripture is connecting the dots, so to speak. What we find when we do this is what theologians call "the economy of God." God has a consistent pattern of action, and he reveals himself to be the same type of person yesterday, today, and forever. The spiritual sense of Scripture is based on this truth. That is why we can connect the work of Jesus with the exodus and the flood, for example.

However, this economy of God is not detectable to those who focus only on the words. As a result, most Biblicists deny that an economy of God exists, or they downplay its importance. They don't look for types of Christ or connections between the various episodes in the Bible. Indeed, the spiritual sense of Scripture is regarded with suspicion in most fundamentalist circles. One of the main reasons for this is that attempts at finding a spiritual meaning of Scripture while focusing on only the words of the text can get silly in a hurry.

For example, I recently ran into a YouTube clip in which it was suggested that Jesus actually revealed the name of the Antichrist when he told his disciples, "I beheld Satan as lightning fall from heaven" (Luke 10:18 KJV). Who is it? According to the anonymous producer, it's Barack Obama. In an interview with an online newsmagazine, the self-described Christian theologian explained: "When I started doing a little research, I found the Greek word for 'lightning' is *astrape,* and the Hebrew equivalent is *Baraq.*"[29] He then focused on the word *heaven* and found that it could be interpreted "the heights" or "high places."

He then recalled Isaiah 14:14, where Lucifer, another name for Satan, is quoted as saying, "I will ascend above the heights of the clouds; I will be like the most High." "I wondered what the word *heights* is," said PPSimmons, "and I looked it up in the dictionary, and it's *Bamah.*"

Thus, on the video, the announcer notes, "If spoken by a Jewish rabbi today, influenced by the poetry of Isaiah, he would say these words in Hebrew . . . 'I saw Satan as Baraq Ubamah.'"

"Gosh, was Jesus giving us a clue, or was this just a freak coincidence?" thought the filmmaker at the time of his research.[30]

It was neither. What we have here is a case of ridiculous hermeneutics. The producer made a huge number of faulty steps here, but for our purposes, let's note two of the most foundational: He didn't establish what the texts actually meant to their authors (he didn't find the literal sense), and in trying to come up with a "spiritual" interpretation he focused only on the words, not the events to which the words point. Most skeptics will look at this video, be affirmed in their skepticism, and think themselves all the wiser for rejecting Christianity.

Conclusion

The goal of evangelism is not to get people to accept the Bible as true or inerrant or even the Word of God, although I am convinced that Scripture is all of those. The goal of evangelism is to get people to know God. The Bible is intended to help them do that. However, when we treat it as something it is not, such as a magic fax from heaven that must be accepted completely literally, it often has the effect of actually keeping people away from God. Biblicists tend to be motivated by a desire to make sure the Bible is not degraded or treated in a manner unworthy of the Word of God. Unfortunately, and ironically, in their attempt to exalt it to its proper place, they have actually undermined Scripture and kept it from accomplishing its purpose.

When talking with a skeptic, it is important to clarify where the Bible fits within the grand scheme of God's revelation and how to read it properly. This will save you hours of needless debate over so-called Bible difficulties.

PART 3

Dealing With the Data

//////////// **9**

The God Hypothesis

The rest of the book is about comparing and evaluating world-views. As I argued in section 1, you shouldn't venture into this part of a conversation until you have done your best to clarify the skeptic's worldview and helped her better understand the true Christian story. In other words, before you start debating worldviews, you need to have a fairly clear picture of the propositions that are under scrutiny. That doesn't mean that the skeptic needs to be able to recite back all the theology we covered in section 2, but she should be able to sum up the Christian story as a three- or four-part drama.

The main points in the story of Christianity can be divided into Creation, the Fall, Redemption (Ongoing New Creation), and the Final New Creation. God created us out of love and for love, but we use our freedom to love the creation rather than the Creator and put ourselves out of touch with reality. Thankfully, God in his grace made a way for us to be created again through Jesus. We eagerly await and work toward the consummation of that process.

When you are satisfied that the skeptic has a somewhat decent grasp of those basics and that you understand the essentials of his worldview, you can move on to debate which theory of reality is more likely to be true.

Frankly, you may never get to this point in most conversations, and that's all right. When I was younger, my conversations with skeptics were almost entirely argumentative. I skipped right over all the foundational stuff and went right to the debate. Now many of the discussions I take part in don't have any debating in them at all. We spend most of our talk just trying to correct faulty views of Christianity. Indeed, sometimes that takes many discussions. I have mentioned in this book only a few of the more common errors, but there are hundreds more. One could take weeks and months with an unbeliever just trying to undo his misconceptions about Christianity. It simply makes no sense to rush into a debate if the skeptic doesn't have a clear view of the gospel.

You may even find that debate is not necessary at all. After hearing a sound view of Christianity, some people will realize they have been rejecting a view of the faith that is not as universal as they thought, and will want some time to mull over the new information and consider Jesus again. Admittedly, this probably won't happen very often, especially among the more vocal and aggressive skeptics, but it can. I've experienced it many times over the years.

Other folks may realize they don't reject Christianity based on the arguments anyway. For example, in August 2011, I took a call from a guy named Jason. He had been in ministry for twenty-five years before leaving Christianity to become a self-described "secular humanist." As we talked, it became clear that he had not abandoned the faith for intellectual reasons. Near the end of the conversation, after I had explained my view of God's nature and purposes, he blurted out angrily: "If Christianity was about God loving us and us loving God, I would still be a Christian."[1] There was really no sense in moving on to argue about whether Jason's new worldview was more likely to be true than Christianity. He hadn't rejected the God of the Bible because he thought Christianity was false, he had rejected him because he didn't think God loved him. That was the point we needed to talk about.

However, some, perhaps most conversations do need to move on to an argument (in the philosophical sense of the word, not the emotional sense) about why we should or should not accept one worldview over another. How are we to do that? In this chapter we will look briefly at some criteria for worldview evaluation and offer some tips on how to effectively direct the conversation where you want it to go.

First, though, a quick note on the model of apologetics I present in this book. It is not the only way to do evangelism or apologetics. However, I am convinced that it is a good and biblical way that works well in today's culture. So I practice it and encourage others to do the same. I love what Groothuis has to say in this regard:

> Much ink has been spilled over apologetic methodology. Various schools have contended that their way is superior to others. Some apologists have spent as much or more time attempting to refute their fellow apologists' methods than they have in attempting to bring apologetics to the people who need it most: unbelievers and doubting followers of Jesus. Evangelist Dwight L. Moody was once criticized by another Christian for his approach to evangelism. Moody's response was that he liked the way he did evangelism better than the way his critics didn't do evangelism. This lesson applies to apologetic method as well.[2]

Also, let's admit that there simply is no foolproof method of reasoning that will work with everyone, or even most people. As Mitch Stokes correctly points out,

Reasoning in real life . . . is extremely complicated, and we can't artificially distill it to a neat and simple method. . . . More goes into evaluating arguments than our beliefs and the logical relations between them. Our emotions and desires, our likes and dislikes, often influence which new beliefs we're willing to take on.[3]

However, that doesn't mean we shouldn't try to reason with people. There is a group within Christianity that rejects apologetics altogether. I think they are simply wrong. We are reasoning creatures, and as we saw in chapter 2, God certainly tries to use apologetics with us. He presents evidence that is intended to lead us to certain conclusions. "Come now, let us reason together," says the Lord in Isaiah 1:18 RSV. J. P. Moreland writes,

Regularly, the prophets appealed to evidence to justify belief in the biblical God or in the divine authority of their inspired message: fulfilled prophecy, the historical fact of miracles, the inadequacy of finite pagan deities to be a cause of such a large, well-ordered universe compared to the God of the Bible, and so forth. They did not say, "God said it, that settles it, you should believe it!" They provided a rational defense for their claims.[4]

Groothuis adds that Jesus himself was a brilliant thinker and an apologist who debated his interrogators with exceptional intellectual skill and acumen.

Jesus deftly employed a variety of reasoning strategies in His debates on various topics. These include escaping the horns of a dilemma, *a fortiori* arguments, appeals to evidence, and *reductio ad absurdum* arguments. Jesus' use of persuasive arguments demonstrates that He was both a philosopher and an apologist who rationally defended His worldview in discussions with some of the best thinkers of His day.[5]

The apostles also made great use of apologetics. They worked hard to "demolish arguments and every pretension that sets itself up against the knowledge of God" (2 Corinthians 10:5) and to make sure no one was taken captive by "hollow and deceptive philosophy" (Colossians 2:8–9). They also admonished their followers to contend for the faith entrusted to them (Jude 3). Paul's discourse on Mars Hill (Acts 17:22–31) is considered by many to be a blueprint for apologetics.

Those who object to apologetics often assert that no one gets argued into Christianity. People believe based on their hearts, not their heads, it is claimed, or based on a direct experience of God. They never get reasoned into the kingdom.

First, this is simply not true. Some people, such as C. S. Lewis, do become followers of Jesus based largely on the arguments for theism and Christianity[6] (more on this in chapter 13). Also, write Kreeft and Tacelli, even if the heart moves people more than the head, "apologetics gets at the heart *through* the head. The head is important precisely because it is a gate to the heart. We can only love what we know."[7]

Groothuis notes, "Although reasoning with unbelievers can prove frustrating, this may be more the fault of poor arguments, poor presentations or poor character than of the fruitlessness of apologetics per se."[8] Skeptics already have enough obstacles to hurdle in order to get to God. They don't need anti-intellectualism thrown in their paths as well. Believers can and should welcome apologetics as a helpful tool in bringing people to Jesus.

Worldview Evaluation

In *Christian Apologetics: A Comprehensive Case for Biblical Faith*, Groothuis presents a model of apologetics he refers to as "worldview hypothesis evaluation and verification." In this approach, "the Christian worldview is taken as a large-scale hypothesis (or metanarrative) that attempts to explain what matters most."[9] This nicely sums up what we talked about in chapter 1. We are to understand Christianity as a "broad-ranging theory of everything, in that it tries to account for the nature and meaning of the universe and its inhabitants"[10] and compare it to other belief systems that do the same in order to discover which worldview is most likely to be true. Through a variety of arguments, we can show that Christianity alone makes the most sense of what matters most and is therefore superior to its rivals.

Groothuis notes that some might object that the term *hypothesis* doesn't seem right in describing the Christian faith, as it is a relationship to a personal God more than a commitment to a list of propositions that may or may not be true. I understand the concern. Certainly I regard my faith in God as more than a hypothesis. However, let's remember that the unbeliever does not yet have that relationship. To him, Christianity is still, at best, just a possibility.[11] We need to help him realize that it is not only possible, but almost certain to be true.

Also, there may be some concern over the idea that we are only trying to figure out which worldview is *most likely* to be true. Can't we have 100 percent proof? Well, not based on the style of apologetics we are recommending in this book. That is not to say that proof is not possible. I think Thomas Aquinas offered some valid proofs of God's existence, for example. It is also not to say that we cannot be certain of God's existence and our relationship with him. The knowledge of God we get from direct experience of him and the indwelling of the Holy Spirit is certainly more than just a probability. However, skeptics don't have that and we can't force it on them. God does not generally overwhelm people with his presence to the point where their free will is overcome. Rather, he woos and persuades and proclaims, using evidences and arguments to back up his message. That is what we are trying to do as well. The type of argument presented in this book does not offer certainty to skeptics who don't yet know Jesus, but it can help them in the right direction.

So how do we go about doing that? Here are a few guidelines for comparing and evaluating worldviews.

A Worldview Should Have Explanatory Power

As we have already established, a worldview is a theory about the nature of reality. As with any theory, we should measure the viability of a worldview by its explanatory power. A worldview must be able to adequately and comprehensively deal with the data. It must be able to account for life as we experience it every day.

The idea that a theory should have explanatory power is a staple of detective stories and scientific research, but it is also used by everyone every day. Philosophers call it inference to the best explanation. It works like this: When faced with certain facts (pieces of data we know to be true), we posit a theory to explain those facts or at least shop around for a theory that could do it. The theory that best accounts for the data is the one we should accept.

For example, just yesterday I found a football lying in the middle of our backyard that I had never seen before. What could account for this phenomenon? I quickly went through a few theories.

Perhaps my wife purchased the ball for our kids while I was at work. That would account for the ball's presence in the yard, but it wouldn't easily make sense of the fact that the ball looked weathered and well used, so I moved on to another theory.

Could it be that the ball came from one of my children's friends? Maybe it was a gift, or some kid left it at our house by mistake. That would explain the presence and condition of the ball. However, I also knew that my children hadn't been with their friends that day and don't usually play football anyway. So this theory also had some weaknesses. It could explain the data, but was unsupported by any corroborating evidence and therefore seemed less than plausible.

In the end I went with a third theory: Perhaps the children from next door had accidentally thrown their old football over the fence. This theory didn't seem to stumble at any level; it explained all the data and was supported by the evidence of my previous experience. The neighbor kids love to throw things around, and we have a long history of sending Frisbees, balls, and other items back over to them. I didn't have 100 percent proof that my theory was correct. However, in light of the data that I had available, the "neighbor" theory was superior to the others in that it explained all the data and was supported by outside evidence. Put another way, the third theory was the most plausible because it didn't require that I ignore any of the data or go to great unwarranted lengths to stretch my theory to make it fit.

For example, let's say I really wanted to believe that my wife bought the football that day. However, the football clearly seemed to have been used for more than one afternoon. I could add some more levels of detail to my theoretical story to make it work out. I could posit that my wife bought the ball at a used sporting goods store, for example. That would account for its location and its appearance. Or how about this for a theory: My wife bought a new ball but then she and the kids took it to a gravel pit and ran over it several times with the SUV. That would explain the data as well. However, adding unsupported claims to the theory makes it much less plausible. Do I have any evidence that they drove over the ball with a truck? No. Is it likely that my wife shopped at a used sporting goods store for the very first time in her life to buy something the kids wouldn't really enjoy? Not really. The theory is becoming shakier by the minute. The more unsupported and improbable propositions I have to accept in order for a theory to account for the data, the less likely a theory is to be true, especially if there are competing theories that account for the data just as well.

So we should go with the theory that (a) accounts for all or most of the data (it doesn't have to ignore the data or leave it unexplained) and (b) does so with stories supported by evidence. After all, it's very easy to come up with a story that explains the data. I could have theorized that an eagle carried the football from another state and dropped it in my backyard. Or it was beamed down from the starship *Enterprise*. Or we all live in the Matrix and the ball wasn't really there. The data can always be explained. The key is to explain it without resorting to a *just so story*[12] that lacks any evidence whatsoever. As Greg Koukl points out, "It's not uncommon for someone to say, 'Oh, I can explain that,' and then conjure up a story that supports her view. But . . . giving an explanation is not the same as giving an argument—or refuting someone else's argument."[13]

Perhaps history's most famous example of inference to the best explanation is the Copernican revolution in astronomy. As measuring equipment became more sophisticated and accurate during the Middle Ages, more and more data came to light that caused problems for the Ptolemaic idea that the earth was fixed at the center of the universe. For example, that model couldn't readily explain why some planets seem to retrograde (reverse their direction of orbit for a time before returning to their original pattern). To account for this fact, Ptolemaic scholars developed increasingly complex geocentric models. They postulated that the sun and moon orbited around the earth, but the rest of the planets and stars orbited around the sun while embedded in invisible spheres that rotated around other invisible spheres that rotated around other invisible spheres, and so on. These complex theories explained more of the data (not all), but astronomers really had to stretch it to make it work. There was an unwieldy amount of math involved in predicting planetary motions, and even then the model wasn't entirely accurate. Copernicus, on the other hand, suggested a model that explained the data more simply and predicted the planetary motion much more precisely. Thus, his view that the planets orbited the sun rightly won out as the superior theory. It had much greater explanatory power.

We can evaluate worldviews the same way. There are many worldviews that can account for the data. That is not the issue. The issue is which one *best* accounts for the data. Which story of the world has to ignore the evidence or stretch to great lengths to make it fit? As we will see in the examples of the next few chapters, the Christian worldview holds up much better than the others.

Other Criteria for Evaluating Worldviews

There are also many other criteria that can be used to evaluate worldviews. For example, a worldview should be logically consistent. If the essential elements of a worldview are self-contradictory, it is false. Also, one should be able to live according to the tenets of one's worldview. Many people deny that objective morality exists, yet they certainly don't live that way. In *Christian Apologetics*, Groothuis also offers six other excellent criteria for evaluating worldviews. They include coherence (if the essential elements of a worldview are meaningfully interconnected conceptually, it is more likely to be true than if its propositions are not connected in this way) and factual adequacy (the claims of a worldview must not contradict historical and empirical facts about reality).[14] Groothuis does a masterful job in this area and I encourage you to check out his book.

Again, we will see examples of how to apply these criteria in the following chapters. Before we get to that, however, a few practical tips for comparing worldviews with skeptics.

Dealing With the Data

First, it is important that you each agree on the nature of the data that needs to be explained. You need to establish a point of discussion at which you are both comfortable starting. For example, if I were to enter into a debate with someone about the best explanation for the football in my backyard, we would both have to agree on some of the basic facts of the case. Can we both accept that the ball was there? Do we both agree that the ball had not previously been a part of the family sports equipment inventory? How about the idea that it looked old—can we agree on that? If we can agree on some or all of these points, then off we go. However, if there is a dispute as to the nature of the data, then that has to be established first. If the other person does not accept that the ball looked used (or whatever), then we either need to establish the facts of the case in regard to the appearance of the ball or not allow that alleged piece of data into the discussion at all.

This is very important when discussing data with a skeptic. You need to establish a starting point on which you both agree. If you present as fact that *the Bible is the inspired Word of God* as your piece of evidence, and then try to build your case for a Christian worldview from there, it simply won't work. The skeptic isn't going to accept biblical inspiration as fact. You need something that he can agree is true. In the same way, the unbeliever can't present as fact that *matter is all that exists.* You won't accept that. Neither side should present as evidence something that the other side thinks still needs to be proven.

To accomplish this, you may have to take some time to establish the facts of the case. For example, if one of the pieces of data presented by the skeptic is an assertion that *the New Testament was written 400 years after Jesus,* you will obviously reject that as false. Either you can debate that idea or the skeptic can choose to leave it and try to find something you do accept.

In the same way, if you start your argument for a Christian worldview with the proclamation that *the tomb was empty* and the unbeliever does not accept that, you will have to try to establish that as a fact. This can get cumbersome and leave you easily sidetracked, which is why I don't recommend presenting such a claim in your initial argument.

A List of Indisputable Facts

Indeed, I don't recommend presenting just one claim. Rather, present a quick list of evidences that you think are much better explained by Christianity than any other worldview. This list should include pieces of data that most people will find impossible to deny. For example, I always include as part of my initial package of evidences the fact that *the New Testament exists* and *the church exists.* We have the document and we have believers, right here, right now. No one can deny this. What is the best explanation for their current existence? I think you can work from these two truths to defend the reliability of Scripture and the historicity of the resurrection of Christ and build a very strong case for Christianity from two easy-to-affirm pieces of data. However, I don't just rest my case on those two pieces. I also include several other facts, including:

- claims of personal experience of God ("mystical" experiences, character transformation, etc.)
- claims of divine intervention into everyday life in the form of "providential" occurrences
- miracle claims, particularly physical healings
- the existence of evil in the world
- the existence of good in the world
- the reliability of reason
- claims of encounters with supernatural powers
- humankind's experience of longing
- humankind's experience of choosing (exercising free will)
- our experience of being conscious
- our experience of having a conscience
- the fact that all children believe in non-physical personhood and purpose in life
- the overarching unfolding of history, particularly in regard to Israel
- the universe seems to be designed
- the universe seems to have a purpose
- the apparent fulfillment of prophecy
- the nature of near-death experiences
- humankind's experience of beauty

This is not an exhaustive list by any means, but presenting it performs a very handy function: It sends the message that you do not base your case for Christianity on one or two disputable claims. Rather, it is based on a large variety of verifiable and widely known facts about the world we live in. Certainly some of these may be denied by the skeptic, but by and large they are not very controversial in and of themselves. The data is accepted. How that data is explained is the controversial thing.

For example, notice that *I don't claim* that people interact with supernatural powers (although I certainly think that they do). Rather, I base my case on the fact that *people claim* to interact with them. I don't state as a fact that we have free will; I state that *it seems like* we have free will. By doing this, I can almost always reach an agreement with the skeptic as to the nature of the data. We can agree that people have near-death experiences, for example. We might disagree as to how to explain them, but the fact of the phenomenon itself is not in dispute. When it comes to the Bible, I don't claim up front that it is trustworthy or divine or anything else that the skeptic will immediately deny. Rather, I build my case for those other truths from a starting point that everyone can agree on.

I realize that this may seem like silly semantic games. After all, in the course of the discussion I will still have to defend the idea that the Bible is trustworthy, and people actually do interact with angels and demons, and that they really do make free choices. Shouldn't we just jump to that right away? I don't think so. Practically speaking, conversations go much more smoothly if you can establish a point of agreement from which to build. There is a big difference between saying, "I believe people have free will; you don't agree; let's debate the issue" and saying, "We both agree that it seems like people make free choices. What is the best explanation for this phenomenon? You present your case, and I'll present mine." The latter statement will produce much better results. Again, we could frame the discussion by saying, "I think we are created for God; you don't agree; let's argue this thing out." But it is better to say, "We can agree, I suspect, that people constantly long for something more. Nothing seems to satisfy us completely. What is the best explanation for this phenomenon? You present your theory, and I'll present mine."

The Skeptic's Data

With regard to the claims that the skeptic might present as evidence for her worldview, it is important to get her to present *a positive case for her worldview* rather than merely *a negative case against yours*. One key is to ask the right questions. For instance, ask for evidence or data that she thinks supports her worldview. Don't ask, "What reasons do you have for believing Christianity isn't true?" or something similar that will keep you on the defensive. Rather, encourage the skeptic to think like a lawyer who has you on the jury. Have her make a positive case: "What can you show me that would convince me that you have the better theory of reality than the Christian?" "What evidence do you have that is better explained by your worldview?"

Sometimes you will be able to accept the evidence at face value and explain it from a Christian perspective. For example, here are some data points that might be offered that are certainly true:

- There is evil in the world.
- Christians have moral failings.
- Science is reliable in describing and predicting natural phenomenon.
- There are many religions in the world.
- There are similarities between the Gospels and pagan myths.

A Christian can accept these propositions as true and explain them from within a Christian worldview in a way that is superior to rival explanations.

Other propositions can't be accepted. For example:

- The Bible is unreliable.
- There is no evidence for God.
- Supernatural experiences don't happen today.

If the skeptic is basing his position on these alleged facts, then you will have to dispute them. There is a third category of data that the unbeliever might present that falls into a bit of a gray area between the other two. This would include propositions such as "The universe is much older than 6,000 years." Some Christians agree that this statement is true, while others don't. Because I believe that you can be a good Christian while being on either side of this issue, I generally don't debate it with unbelievers. That is not to say that I don't have a position or that this topic is not important, it's just that I don't think it is worth being dogmatic about with a skeptic. Whatever you believe about the age of the universe, the skeptic does not need to pick a position in order to become a Christian. Therefore, we shouldn't put up any unnecessary intellectual roadblocks in his way.

This principle also applies to various minor points of doctrine that are not held by all Christians but that can present a stumbling block to an unbeliever if he thinks it is mandatory to accept them as part of the Christian package. For example, I don't think you should discuss your church's particular views on the exercise of spiritual gifts as part of a worldview discussion with an unbeliever.

Before Moving On

A quick note about the subjects I will discuss in the next three chapters: They do not represent a comprehensive case for the Christian worldview or against any other worldview. They are not even necessarily the best evidences for either side of the debate. They are samples of some of the subjects that you might talk about with a skeptic. Also, please realize that I am not dealing with even the topics I reference here in a comprehensive way; I am only offering a brief overview of the arguments. There are dozens, if not hundreds, of wonderful apologetics resources available that offer evidences and arguments in support of Christianity, and I did not think it was necessary (or possible) to restate or reference them all here. Rather, I picked three pieces of evidence that I believe are important and powerful, especially in our culture, and that don't always receive the attention they deserve in books on this subject. My goal is primarily to give you some examples of how to deal with the data when using worldview hypothesis evangelism. Obviously I hope that you will be better equipped and more willing to use the arguments presented here, but I'm more concerned that you are better equipped to effectively use the arguments presented in all those other wonderful books and resources. This is a template for dealing with the data, not an encyclopedia of what to say when faced with the data.

We will start with a piece of evidence that is usually presented by skeptics as evidence that Christianity is false and then move to two facts that you can present as evidence that it is true.

Christianity and Pagan Myths

Jesus as Myth

For fifty-seven years, Christmas in Santa Monica, California, included a two-block long display of nativity scenes, each depicting a different event from the story of the birth of Christ. Residents and tourists alike made a tradition of strolling slowly past the enclosures in Palisades Park. Well, most of them did. Not everyone was happy with the situation. In 2011 Raymond McNeely made national news when he won a lottery and got control of nine of the vandal-proof boxes. Instead of setting up Mary, Joseph, and the shepherds, however, McNeely left six of his containers empty while placing anti-Christian messages in the other three. One read RELIGIONS ARE ALL ALIKE—FOUNDED UPON FABLES AND MYTHOLOGIES.—THOMAS JEFFERSON. HAPPY SOLSTICE, proclaimed another. A third contained photographs depicting King Neptune, Jesus, Santa Claus, and the devil with the caption, 37 MILLION AMERICANS KNOW MYTHS WHEN THEY SEE THEM. WHAT MYTHS DO

YOU SEE?[1] That sign was sponsored by American Atheists, an organization well known for renting billboards with similar messages, including YOU KNOW IT'S A MYTH. THIS SEASON, CELEBRATE REASON!

McNeely's view is gaining steam in our culture, and may well be a topic you will have to address when talking with skeptics. If you have been able to frame the conversation as a worldview discussion, the unbeliever may point to the similarity between the Christian story and ancient myths that preceded it as evidence that Christianity is just one more of those myths.

As Rene Girard points out, "From the earliest days of Christianity, the Gospels' resemblance to certain myths has been used as an argument against Christian faith."[2] In his book *Jesus Potter Harry Christ*, Derek Murphy presents one of the latest incarnations of that argument. After documenting how the story of Jesus has similar characteristics to the tales of Gilgamesh, Dionysus, Pythagorus, Orpheus, Mithras, and many other gods, he concludes "that Christian writers assimilated elements from paganism into the Christian mythos."[3]

The idea that the gospel writers invented a fictional character that goes far beyond the "Jesus of history" is widespread. Murphy represents an increasingly large and vocal group of skeptics who think that the gospel writers made up the character of Jesus by drawing from other myths.

Their basic argument is this: We know that the ancient myths were false. They were not historical accounts, but rather tall tales made up by primitive and ignorant people trying to make sense of a world they didn't understand and couldn't control. They are pious inventions arising from the imaginations of the storytellers themselves. The Jesus story is similar to these myths. Therefore, the Jesus story is likely a myth with the same cause rather than an actual historical account.

Step One: Clarify the Data

So we have the skeptic's data and his explanation. The first step is to clearly establish the facts of the case and make sure we agree on the nature of the data. Is there actually a similarity between Christianity and the myths of ancient cultures and religions? If so, what is the nature of the parallels and just how close are they? After we have settled on some point of agreement about the facts, we can move on to critique the skeptic's explanation of those facts and offer a more satisfying one of our own.

Parallels Between Christianity and Ancient Myths

Many Christians try to counter the skeptic's claim that Christianity is just another myth by denying that there are any substantial similarities between other stories and the Gospels at all. This is a mistake. The truth is that most skeptics could go much farther than they do in exploring parallels between cultural and religious myths and the biblical narrative. There are many levels of correspondence between Christianity and pagan[4] tales and legends. Let's take Plato's famous parable of the cave as an example.

In the story, slaves are chained in darkness for their entire lives, forced to stare at a wall. The only light comes from a fire burning behind them that casts shadows on the wall whenever objects pass between the slaves and the fire. The slaves assume that the shadows are reality. Then one slave escapes and discovers the truth. After seeing the beauty and solidity of the outside world, he returns to testify to the light. He reports that the shadows are just images of things much more real. Angrily, the slaves kill the prophet, assuming he is making fun of them. Many elements of this story are hardly unique to Plato. As David Marshall points out,

169

The pattern of a hero who descends into the earth to rescue those trapped in darkness, facing death to deliver those without hope, appears again and again in both ancient and modern mythology.[5]

For example, notes Marshall, Orpheus traveled to Hades to rescue his lost love; Chinese Buddhist saint Miao Shan freed prisoners chained in the underworld; and the Egyptian god Isis rescued Osiris, god of the Nile, from death at the hand of the god Set. Even contemporary film heroes such as James Bond and Indiana Jones are known for descending into the very heart of darkness to rescue those in peril.[6] We could go on and on, of course. Frodo and Sam enter the black land of Mordor to throw the One Ring into Mount Doom and save the world from the evil Sauron. Luke Skywalker offers himself into the hands of the dark lord Darth Vader in order to rescue his friends on Endor and save the Rebel Alliance. All these stories parallel Jesus in that he sacrificed himself in order to proclaim the truth and rescue those trapped in darkness and slavery. In this, Derek Murphy is quite right to compare Jesus to Harry Potter as well. And this is just one level of similarity.

Indeed, let's expand the data pool in this area (and potentially give the skeptic some more ammunition) by pointing out that there are many other ways in which the beliefs and practices of ancient cultures and religions find common ground with Christianity.

For example, the idea of atonement, "a substitution of something offered, or some personal suffering, for a penalty which would otherwise be exacted,"[7] seems to be as old as history itself. "The practice of atonement is remarkable for its antiquity and universality, proved by the earliest records that have come down to us of all nations, and by the testimony of ancient and modern travelers."[8]

Even the symbols that ancient people used to represent meta-physical and supernatural concepts have parallels in Christianity. In *The Sacred and the Profane*, an authoritative treatise on the use of myth, symbol, and ritual in religion, Mircea Eliade notes that religious symbols have a remarkable uniformity across all cultures and times.

For example, the earth (as in dirt, *terra firma*) has everywhere been understood as the mother of all things, the womb from which man proceeds. And water is universally associated with both death and rebirth. Immersion in water is seen as a return to the primordial chaos and is equivalent to death, while at the same time being the source of fertilization and regeneration of life.[9] These ideas are certainly not foreign to biblical religion. Adam was born of the dust of the ground, and as we have already studied in this book, water is a means of destroying evil and at the same time bringing forth new life at creation, the flood, the crossing of the Red Sea, and, of course, baptism. Eliade also details the universal symbolism of many other physical objects, including the sun, sky, serpents, and even rocks.[10]

So we can affirm with the skeptic that there are similarities between Christianity and other ancient religious beliefs and practices, even beyond the connections they usually make.

Step Two: Evaluate the Skeptic's Claim

Having established the facts, it's time to move on to evaluate the skeptic's claim and offer the Christian explanation for the data. There is no set order for these two steps, although sometimes the situation may lend itself to one or the other. For example, if the skeptical claim is clearly self-contradictory or full of fac-tual errors, you may want to point that out before offering the Christian position. However, I don't follow a hard and fast rule in this regard. Also, these steps usually overlap; evaluating the skeptic's account and explaining the Christian understanding go together. I've labeled this section Step Two, but that is only to help clarify for you the steps we are taking; it is not meant to be a dogmatic formula.

Mythical Does Not Mean Unhistorical

The skeptic's argument is that all myths are unhistorical and therefore the Jesus story is unhistorical too. Let's start with a quick point of logic. Even if we grant that ancient pagan myths are unhistorical, that does not mean every story that is similar to those myths is unhistorical. In other words, just because a story sounds like something out of a movie script does not mean that it never actually happened.

For example, Michael Phelps won eight gold medals at the 2008 Beijing Olympics in a fashion that would have seemed corny and unbelievable if it had been written into the plot of your average Disney film. But it happened. Events with mythical elements happen all the time. We talked above about the hero who sacrifices himself on behalf of those in slavery and darkness. You don't have to look far into history to find a whole bunch of those types of people in real life:

> A frail Hindu lawyer fasts the British empire into submission while in jail. A Baptist preacher shakes prison dust off his suit and wins African Americans the right to be treated with respect. Both heroes . . . pay for their ambitions with their lives. A Filipino senator, imprisoned, then exiled, returns home and dies for the liberty of his island nation. An African statesman emerges from decades in prison, shaky and pale, to overthrow apartheid and bring racial reconciliation to a nation on the verge of civil war. An army officer turned novelist is released from the Gulag and prays to God to "make me a sword to smite the forces of evil."

He strikes the Evil Empire with his pen, and it withers and dies like a dragon in a fairy tale. These epics of national death and resurrection did not occur in an obscure corner or in a Hans Christian Andersen tale; they defined the twentieth century. They remind us that sometimes, myths come to life. And when they do, society itself may be reborn.[11]

As such, it just doesn't follow that the story of Jesus must be unhistorical simply because it sounds like some stories that are. This is the logical fallacy that traps those believers who expend so much energy trying to disavow any similarity between pagan myths and Christianity. Their attempts are simply not necessary.

Unbelievers also fall prey to this problem. Many skeptics seem to think that the similarities between other cultural beliefs and Christianity prove that Christianity is not true. Bishop Fulton Sheen points out that one of the major false assumptions people make in regard to the study of comparative religions is to believe that "divine and true religion must be different from all other human religions. Since the Christian and non-Christian religions are not absolutely different, in all details, it is falsely concluded that the Christian religion is not divine."[12] Again, this does not follow. This does not mean that the Jesus story is true, of course, but it leaves the door open to the possibility. That prospect becomes more likely when we consider a little more closely some other aspects of the skeptic's claim.

The Jewishness of Jesus

One key to the "Jesus is another myth" position is the assertion that the gospel writers didn't really expect their readers to take the stories literally. The idea is that the authors of the New Testament weren't lying about Jesus so much as they were creating, in the words of Robert Price, a "pious fraud" that used

Jesus as a "euphemistic fiction" in the same way that McDonald's uses Ronald McDonald and the Walt Disney Corporation uses Mickey Mouse.[13] In this view, Jesus was intended to be the embodiment of spiritual principles and sound worldly wisdom rather than an actual historical figure. Unfortunately, according to Price and those who share his position, readers have had it wrong for 2,000 years.

This proposition has many huge holes in it, but I'll focus on just one: Jesus is presented as the *Jewish Messiah*. The gospel writers, regardless of their various audiences and theological emphasis, were unanimous in arguing that Jesus was the fulfillment of the Jewish hope for a savior. That is to say, the gospel authors all saw Jesus as the ultimate end to which all of Jewish history had been leading. Consequently, the writers could not have been intending for their readers to take the accounts of Jesus as nonhistorical because that would be meaningless within the context of Jewish theology. No Jew would accept it.

As we have seen throughout this book, the God of the Jews is not a God who speaks mystically and vaguely about principles for successful living. He is a God who breaks into history and acts in time and space. Jews did not worship a set of ideals, but a God who had called a specific person, Abraham; built him into an actual genetic, physical entity, a family of humans; brought that family out of Egypt from literal slavery at a specific point in time with great physical signs and wonders; defeated other nations in battles that spilled real human blood; and established a political kingdom on earth led by an actual, physical person named David.

These events were not viewed as parables or inspirational myths. They were understood as God's hand in history, and it was on the historicity of these events that the Jews placed their hope for the future. They were expecting God to act again because he had done so in the past. They were looking forward to a time when God would again break into history and redeem them from their current state of slavery. If those past events didn't actually happen, the Jews had no god to worship and no hope for a Messiah. They put their faith in a person, not a set of ideals (read Psalms, for example).

As such, to present a nonhistorical savior to the Jews, which is what these "Jesus as Myth" scholars say happened, would be ridiculous. A savior who didn't act in time and space would be no savior at all.

Of course, it is clear that the New Testament writers did intend their readers to see Jesus as historical. For example, look at the sermons as recorded in the beginning of Acts: Peter (Acts 2:14–41) and Stephen (Acts 7:2–53) both concentrate their sermons about Jesus on the fact that God has worked in the past and has now worked in history again. They clearly did not see Jesus as a nonhistorical myth.

Step Three: Offer the Christian Explanation of the Data

Christian orthodoxy is not threatened by the existence of pagan myths that are similar to the Gospels. Indeed, the existence and nature of those myths simply lends more credibility to the claims of Christianity. In this section we will examine how Christianity explains the parallels between itself and other traditions. We will also see that, even as it is similar in many ways, Christianity differs from and transcends the pagan stories and religions.

Unhistorical Does Not Mean Completely False

The foundation of the skeptic's argument is that pagan myths are false. They build from the idea "We know that every god in the pagan pantheon is completely imaginary" to suggest that

Jesus was imaginary too. The first point to make in explaining the Christian approach to pagan myths is to point out that they are not *completely* imaginary. Let's talk for a moment about the source of pagan myths.

Skeptics suggest that religious myths are humanity's poor attempt to explain the world and our place in it. The stories are primitive and ignorant people's attempt to answer the big questions of life. Humans didn't know how the universe works, so they made up a bunch of legends about animals in the sky. There is some truth in this. Certainly many pagan traditions are the result of an effort to describe the "mysterious and mysteriously ordered"[14] reality in which people find themselves.[15]

Humans ask questions and then answer those questions with supernatural myths. However, whereas the skeptic thinks that ancient people failed in their quest to find answers, and the myths are completely false, Christianity asserts that the pagans actually found some right answers to the big questions of life. The myths are not entirely wrong. Ancient people didn't know the full extent of the truth, certainly, but they weren't totally out in left field either. As I expand on this point, we will see how it explains the parallels between Christianity and pagan myths.

Knowledge of God Outside of Israel and the Church

I have argued throughout the book that God's desire is to know and be known. And so he has been revealing himself in the world from the very beginning. We noted in chapter 8 that this involves both interacting directly with people in time and space (special revelation) as well as "pouring forth speech" through creation itself (general revelation). The bottom line, as Francis Schaeffer famously put it, is that "God is there and he is not silent."[16]

From the perspective of the Christian worldview, then, all people have access to some knowledge of the one true God. This might come through reflection on the cosmos or through some interaction with special revelation, for instance stories handed down through generation after generation of a supreme god who acted in times past. So one does not have to be a Jew or a Christian to have understanding of the one true God. Indeed, Scripture itself is full of pagans who knew, albeit sometimes imperfectly, the God of Abraham, Isaac, Jacob, and Jesus.

Perhaps the most famous of these was Melchizedek, the king of the Canaanite city of Salem who was also a priest of El Elyon, or "God most High." Melchizedek brought bread and wine to Abram and blessed him by El Elyon, saying that this God was the maker of heaven and earth (Genesis 14:19) who had defeated Abram's enemies (Genesis 14:20). Abram, a follower of Yahweh (often interpreted in our Bibles as LORD), then tithed to Melchizedek, affirming that he acknowledged Melchizedek's position as a priest. Interestingly, when another character in this story, the king of Sodom, wanted Abram to take the spoils of the battle, Abram refused, saying, "I have sworn to the LORD, God Most High, maker of heaven and earth, that I would not take a thread or a sandal-thong or anything that is yours, so that you might not say, 'I have made Abram rich'" (Genesis 14:21–23 NRSV). Gerald McDermott offers some good insight into this text: "Notice what Abram had done in these words: he identified Yahweh with El Elyon in two ways. He has joined the two names in a gesture that suggests they point to the same God, and—as if it were not completely clear—he has given Melchizedek's description of El Elyon to Yahweh: maker of heaven and earth."[17]

Though Melchizedek lived in Canaan and had a different name for Yahweh, clearly he was worshiping the same God as

Abram. Whether that came from general or special revelation is a matter of debate among Bible scholars,[18] but the point here is that knowledge of God was found apart from Abram and his direct descendants. In other words, the culture in Canaan at the time had some knowledge of Yahweh apart from what he was doing in the main biblical narrative.

This same knowledge was also available to the Greeks living in the sixth century BC. According to solid ancient sources,[19] during this time Athens came under the grip of a terrible plague. After appealing for a solution to the hundreds of gods in the Greek pantheon without success, the leaders of Athens decided to solicit the advice of an outside expert: the Cretan Epimenides. He told the Athenians that they should offer sacrifices to the supreme god who was more powerful than all their local deities. This they did, and in order not to risk offending this god by giving him the wrong name, they set up altars with the inscription TO AN UNKNOWN GOD. By the next morning the plague was receding, and within a week it was gone. It was one of these altars that Paul mentions in Acts 17:

> Paul then stood up in the meeting of the Areopagus and said: "People of Athens! I see that in every way you are very religious. For as I walked around and looked carefully at your objects of worship, I even found an altar with this inscription: TO AN UNKNOWN GOD. So you are ignorant of the very thing you worship—and this is what I am going to proclaim to you."
>
> Acts 17:22–23

Paul accepts that the God to whom the Athenians sacrificed half a millennium earlier is the same God that he is preaching about. He even goes on to quote approvingly from the third century BC poet Aratus: "As some of your own poets have said, 'We are his offspring'" (Acts 17:28). Clearly Paul believed that there was some revelation of the true God even amid all the abhorrent idolatry of Athens.

So our Christian explanation of the parallels between pagan myths and the gospel starts with the proposition that people of pagan cultures do have some knowledge of the one true God, and this is reflected in their myths. If God's revelation is known everywhere, it makes sense that the ancient stories would be infused with at least some of this truth. Jesus is the fullest and clearest expression of God's truth, but other cultures and religions are not completely void of fact.[20]

Why Myths?

Let's answer a couple of questions that might arise at this point. First, if knowledge of God is available to all, why don't the pagan religions proclaim him more clearly? Why do they resort to using myths? The problem, writes Michael Christensen, is that "transcendent reality, when envisioned by the imagination, does not readily adapt itself to interpretation and communication."[21] As finite human beings, constrained by the limits of human language, it is difficult if not impossible for us to conceptualize and express religious experiences and supernatural truths in straightforward and literal terms. "Language can only point to that which cannot be adequately communicated. The reality to which language points must be experienced in order to be known."[22]

The best way to communicate a supernatural truth, according to C. S. Lewis, is myth, because it takes an abstract reality and enables us to experience it. Myth puts a person in touch with ultimate reality in a more intimate way than would be possible simply by knowing what is factual. "In the enjoyment of a great myth we come nearest to experiencing as a concrete what can otherwise be understood only as an abstraction."[23] Properly understood, myths are not about the literal details of the story, as if anyone is supposed to believe that a giant frog actually swallowed up all the waters of the sea. They are about something that can't be described in propositional language. Ancient people used myths not because they were ignorant of natural laws and wanted to try to explain them, but because they wanted to communicate the transcendent truth behind the natural laws, and myths were the best they could do.

The Transcendence of Christianity

The next question to answer is "Are all religions and myths equal, then?" So far I have presented pagan myths in a positive light. Now let's state unequivocally that this does not mean all religions are on par with Christianity. Jesus is absolutely the only way, truth, and life.

Even as it affirms that truth is found in other faiths, *Nostra Aetate* notes that the church is duty-bound to proclaim Christ, "in whom God reconciled all things to himself" and "men find the fullness of their religious life."[24] The last part of that sentence is an important key to understanding orthodox Christianity's approach to other religions: They must be understood in relation to Christ because he is the full self-revelation of God and as such is absolutely unique. Indeed, unique is not an adequate term to describe Christianity, because it insinuates that Christianity is just a myth with different characteristics from the rest. That doesn't quite capture what I am saying here. Christianity is not just a different myth; it is transcendent over other myths. It is a different kind of thing altogether. The myths are humanity's feeble attempt to explain the transcendent. Christianity is the transcendent come down to humans.

As Sheen points out, transcendence

> does not consist in proving that Christianity is better than any other religion, but that it is *above comparison*. Transcendence is a "change of degree, order, and species." . . . Transcendence does not imply that Christianity must bear no resemblance to pagan religions, because similarities do not prove the same cause; nor that Christianity enjoys truth and all other religions are in darkness, but rather that it has historical superiority over them.[25]

Sheen is saying that while pagan myths result, at least in part, from humanity's attempt to understand what I labeled earlier general revelation, Christianity is all about God's special revelation in time and space.

C. S. Lewis refers to the Christian revelation of God coming down to earth in time and space as "myth become fact." In his wonderful sermon "The Weight of Glory," Lewis eloquently summarizes the major theme of this chapter. He writes that if divine revelation is available to all people,

> We should, therefore, expect to find in the imagination of great Pagan teachers and myth makers some glimpse of that theme which we believe to be the very plot of the whole cosmic story— the theme of incarnation, death, and rebirth. And the differences between the Pagan Christs (Balder, Osiris, etc.) and the Christ Himself is much what we should expect to find. The Pagan stories are all about someone dying and rising, either every year, or else nobody knows where and nobody knows when. The Christian story is about a historical personage, whose execution can be dated pretty accurately, under a named Roman magistrate, and with whom the society that He founded is in a continuous relation down to the present day. It is not the difference between falsehood and truth. It is the difference between a real event on the one hand and dim dreams or premonitions of that same event on the other.[26]

The myths of pagan religions and cultures are shadows of the real thing. Christianity is transcendent over religion in that it fulfills religion. This is why Daniélou can state that

> there is, for religious man, no better way of being faithful to his religion than to adhere to revelation. This is why conversion to Christianity is never an infidelity for the pagan. This point should be emphasized over and over again. The pagan will keep all the religious values of his paganism, but he will find in Christ the response that all his desires called for. As St. Paul says, this God for whom he was groping but only through shadows and symbols, this God comes looking for him to give Himself to him, and to reveal to him what he is.[27]

In this vein, Karl Rahner calls Christianity the "absolute religion,"[28] because only Jesus can bring participation in the divine life. He is not just another religious leader, but the one in whom all religions are judged and find their fulfillment. Even though we can find "seeds of the Word" in all religions, Jesus is the savior of all humankind and the only mediator between God and people.[29]

What Went Wrong: The Negative Aspects of Pagan Myths

Before concluding this chapter, let's answer one final question: If pagan myths can correspond to Christian truth and even reveal it, why are the foreign gods often treated so harshly in Scripture and false religions consistently condemned?

We have already seen examples of this in the Bible stories above. Abram was willing to acknowledge that Yahweh and El Elyon were the same, but he refused to grant that this God was on par with the deities of the king of Sodom. Also, Paul did not put the unknown God that he was proclaiming on equal footing with the other gods of Athens. They were clearly inferior and to be abandoned. In our discussion of the Exodus earlier in the book, we saw that God fought against the pagan gods of Egypt and Canaan. How do we reconcile these facts? What went wrong to turn these potentially helpful myths into enemies of the truth? There are many dimensions to the answer, but I'll make three quick points.

First, a problem develops when a culture forgets that the symbol is just a symbol. Idolatry occurs when people worship the sun or the river rather than the One to whom the sun and the river point. The trajectory of this descent is detailed in Romans 1:

> For since the creation of the world God's invisible qualities—his eternal power and divine nature—have been clearly seen, being understood from what has been made, so that men are without excuse.
>
> For although they knew God, they neither glorified him as God nor gave thanks to him, but their thinking became futile and their foolish hearts were darkened. Although they claimed to be wise, they became fools and exchanged the glory of the immortal God for images made to look like mortal man and birds and animals and reptiles. . . . They exchanged the truth of God for a lie, and worshiped and served created things rather than the Creator—who is forever praised.
>
> Romans 1:20–25 niv1984

Second, pagan religions become enemies of God when they fail to yield to the superior revelation of the gospel. Daniélou's insight shines brightly here again:

> The tragedy of religions is . . . wishing to persist once revelation has arrived. . . . We may say that there was a time when Buddha was right . . . that is to say that there was a moment when Buddha, through his experience, in his natural mysticism, interpreted that

which was accessible of God through his revelation in the world. But from the moment when this God whom Buddha was seeking manifested Himself, the precursor, whose very mission was to prepare, has to efface himself. This is why [Romano] Guardini says that Buddha was perhaps a great precursor of Christ, and that he will unquestionably be His final enemy. Thus it was when the Old Testament, which was preparing for Christ, became Judaism, opposed to Christ. Something which has been true can become false, at the precise moment when it becomes outdated.[30]

Third, pagan religions can actually be the worship of false gods. Supernatural beings that hate God and actively work against his purposes do exist. The pagan gods of the Bible are, for the most part, treated as if they are real and have some authority and control. Again, we saw this in the Exodus account, where Pharaoh's magicians had some power, just not enough power. The New Testament affirms this worldview, as Jesus spent much of his ministry casting out demons, and the apostle Paul understood his ministry as a fight against supernatural evil forces that were trying to entice entire cultures to worship them instead of the one true God. As he wrote to the Ephesians: "For our struggle is not against flesh and blood, but against the rulers, against the authorities, against the powers of this dark world and against the spiritual forces of evil in the heavenly realms" (Ephesians 6:12). Indeed, as George Caird points out, "The idea of sinister world powers and their subjugation by Christ is built into the very fabric of Paul's thought, and some mention of it is found in every epistle except Philemon."[31]

Conclusion

The Christian worldview has nothing to fear from the parallels between the gospel and pagan mythology. It can account for the data in a comprehensive and satisfying way. Indeed, Christianity can point to the parallels between all of the religious stories and symbols as evidence against the skeptic's theory. After all, if all myths arise only from people's imaginations, shouldn't they be completely different from place to place around the world? But they aren't. Rather, they have an almost uncanny similarity. The naturalistic view of the origins of religious myth cannot account for this, while the Christian view certainly can. It teaches that the myths are not just the result of people's imaginations, but rather our encounter with objective reality: the universe created by the Christian God.

////////////// **11**

The World Is Not Enough

"Is This All There Is?"

Something went wrong on the way to having it all. I'm in my forties, and many in my age group have now worked long and hard enough to reach the top of their professions. Unfortunately, as Ilya Shapiro writes, "we are not happy. . . . Generation X[1] has arrived, made its presence felt, looked around, and is wondering, 'Is that all there is?'" He notes that even those who seem to have it all are still looking for fulfillment.

> We have everything we could ever want in this stage of life, but still we search for meaning.
>
> Like the government lawyer who tries to have a "parallel life" as a historian. . . . Or the jet-setting consultant who makes films on the side. Or the real estate developer who used to be a filmmaker/banker/musician. . . . These are the people living supposedly perfect lives (or lives on course for perfection) yet feel empty, not being able to find meaning or fulfillment in either materialism or new age spiritualism, Porsches or Pilates.[2]

Perhaps it will get better as we get older, Shapiro hopes at the end of the article. Not likely, suggests baby boomer Gregg Easterbrook. He opens his book *The Progress Paradox: How Life Gets Better While People Feel Worse* with this thought experiment:

> Suppose your great-great grandparents, who lived four generations ago, materialized in the United States of the present day. . . . They would be dazzled. Unlimited food at affordable prices, never the slightest worry about shortage, unlimited variety—strawberries in March!—so much to eat that in the Western nations, overindulgence now plagues not just the well-off but the poor.

Not to mention other aspects of contemporary life that would "strike our recent ancestors as nearly miraculous," such as an almost doubling of the average life, the defeat of history's plagues, the end of backbreaking physical toil for most wage earners, instantaneous global communication, same-day travel to distant cities, the end of formal discrimination, mass homeownership, and incredible advances of freedom. "All told, except for the clamor and speed of society, and for the trends in popular music, your great-great-grandparents might say the contemporary United States is the realization of utopia."[3]

But it isn't utopia. Easterbrook concludes by saying that although everything is better, his generation is also not happy.

> Yet how many of us feel positive about our moment, or even believe that life is getting better? Today Americans tell pollsters that the country is going downhill, that their parents had it better, that they feel unbearably stressed out, that their children face a declining future. . . .
>
> The percentage of Americans who describe themselves as "happy" has not budged since the 1950s, though the typical

person's real income has more than doubled through that period. Happiness has not increased in Japan or Western Europe in the past half-century, either, though daily life in both those places has grown fantastically better, incorporating all the advances noted above plus the end of dictatorships and recovery from war. . . . [Even in an era of abundance and social progress,] the citizens of the United States and the European Union, almost all of whom live better than almost all of the men and women in history, entertain considerable discontent.[4]

If you are looking for a penetrating and thought-provoking fact to drop into your discussion, that is a great place to start. People are not satisfied. Longing for something more is simply a universal fact of life. As we will see in this chapter, this is best explained by the Christian worldview.

The Data of Personal Experience

We spent the previous chapter discussing a fact generally presented by skeptics as evidence against Christianity. Now we'll turn to truths that believers usually introduce into the conversation in support of the Christian worldview. As I mentioned earlier, there is plenty of evidence available, and dozens of good apologetics books that explain the arguments. Feel free to go with whatever topic you feel most comfortable at this stage in the conversation.

However, I suggest that you emphasize (or at least not ignore) the more personal and experiential evidences for Christianity. For example, the Christian worldview offers the best explanation for the universal human experiences of longing (the topic of this chapter), guilt, and the feeling that an unseen power is directing our lives in some way.[5] Christianity also better accounts for more uniquely individual experiences such as mystical encounters

189

with the presence of God, answers to prayer, miraculous healing, encounters with spirits, and direct providential guidance. We'll discuss those experiences in the next chapter.

Here are a couple of reasons to focus on the experiential.

First, it enables you to keep your discussions personal and relevant to everyday life. It's easy to let worldview debates get so academic that they verge on esoteric. You want to avoid that. Evangelistic conversations are not about trying to get the skeptic to sign off on a bunch of abstract facts or even historical propositions; you are trying to bring the unbeliever into a relationship with Jesus. Skeptics need to know more than that God exists or that science supports Christianity, or even that Jesus rose from the dead 2,000 years ago; they need to know that Jesus is living and active in people's lives today.

Of course this assumes that Jesus has changed you for the better and you see how he is active in your life today. I hope that is true. Unfortunately, for many Christians, Jesus is just somebody to believe in, not someone to know personally. Henry Blackaby notes that he was motivated to write his best-selling book *Experiencing God* because he found too many believers

> coming to church every week and learning more and more about God, but they were not *experiencing* Him. To many, He was simply a faraway God to be believed in, a doctrine to affirm, an invisible deity to whom they recited their prayers. They needed to know He is a Person with whom Christians can enjoy an intimate, growing, loving fellowship.[6]

Charles Kraft adds that a major problem with Western Christianity is that it is full of "practicing deists"[7] who treat God as if he were a distant creator who got the universe going but now leaves it to run like a machine. This is a tragedy. As we will discuss in more detail in the next chapter, God is very active in the world today. To miss out on an experiential relationship with God is to miss a wonderful blessing.

This leads to the second reason to focus on the experiential: God not only acts, he acts for our good. I argued in chapter 1 that we shouldn't "sell" the gospel as if it were a consumer product. That does not mean, however, that the truth doesn't provide exactly what people need: love, purpose, meaning, freedom from guilt, and guidance through life, among many other benefits. The gospel is called "good news" for a reason. This is a great time in the conversation to emphasize that. The more you can show the skeptic how the truths you are explaining have had a personal impact on you and can greatly improve his life, the better.

Step One: Present and Clarify the Data

Let's start, as always, by clearly establishing the facts we are presenting. The data on the table in this chapter is that all people feel unfulfilled, and nothing the world offers satisfies their desire for something more. As Doug Groothuis summarizes, "There is, on the one hand, the pained longing for the transcendent and, on the other, the sense of the inadequacy of merely earthly goods to satisfy that longing."[8] People can't find contentment within themselves, they can't find it in other people, and they can't find it in things. That is the problem.

This is not to say that people don't experience moments of happiness and joy, or even that some people are not basically okay with the general state of their lives. We are not claiming that everyone is deeply depressed all the time. We are simply making the point that deep down inside everyone is a metaphysical restlessness that can't be satiated with temporal treasures. Nothing is able to completely satisfy our yearning. No matter how much we gain, the ache remains.

To further clarify, this is not a restlessness that comes from obvious vain pursuits. We are not referring to the guy who sinks all his time and money into collecting string and then wonders why getting his name into the *Guinness Book of World Records* for largest ball of twine isn't more satisfying. The surprising thing about metaphysical restlessness is that it persists even when we pursue worthwhile goals, such as loving relationships and wisdom and the experience of traveling in beautiful and exotic lands. We can gain all the goods the world has to offer and still want more. "There comes a time when one asks even of Shakespeare, even of Beethoven, is this all?"[9]

The Skeptic and the Data

Will the skeptic affirm that universal metaphysical restlessness is a fact? Probably. In my experience, most people are honest and self-aware enough to grant you this one. However, some might reject it, primarily for two reasons.

First, some people simply haven't thought much about it. "I don't know—I'm basically happy," they might respond. However, this view is not the result of any extended or deep reflection on the subject. The sad reality is that many people go through every minute of every day either busy with work and social duties or plugged in to some form of entertainment. Many people simply don't contemplate life's biggest questions, ever. If you can get these folks to actually think about their lives for even a minute, they should realize and admit that life is not all they wish it would be.

Indeed, the fact that people spend their lives so distracted by work and entertainment is evidence, I would suggest, that they aren't content. They don't want to have to think about the pointlessness of it all, and they keep themselves busy so they don't have to. These people don't see entertainment as something restful, recuperative, and contemplative, as it has been traditionally understood, but as an escape from the real world. Why would anyone want to escape from a world in which they are content and happy?[10] Blaise Pascal saw diversion for what it is—an attempt to escape an unpleasant reality marked by inconstancy, boredom, and anxiety.[11]

Just asking "Really?" might be all you need to do here. A moment or two of actual reflection could be enough to get your conversation partner to realize the truth. If she insists that she desires nothing further to make life perfect, you can be almost certain that claim is made only for the sake of her argument with you and not out of deep and honest reflection. No one is completely satisfied with every single aspect of life. If the skeptic insists that she is, it might be best to move on to another point and leave her with her conscience.

A skeptic might also reject your data because he still holds on to the idea that something out there will make him truly content. "If I only had 50 million dollars and a Ferrari and a new supermodel girlfriend every other week, everything would be fine." Peter Kreeft points out,

> The reply to this is, of course, "Try it. You won't like it." It's been tried and has never satisfied. In fact, billions of people have performed and are even now performing trillions of such experiments, desperately seeking the ever-elusive satisfaction they crave. For even if they won the whole world, it would not be enough to fill one human heart.[12]

One doesn't have to be an expert in the history of powerful, rich, and famous people to know that they are no more content than the rest of us. Indeed, the fact that they actually reached the highest rung on society's ladder and still weren't satisfied seems to be partly responsible for the depression and dysfunction that so often accompany this type of success.

You also might take a minute to point out one of the main reasons people find temporal goods unfulfilling: the fact that they are *temporal*. Nothing lasts forever, as the saying goes. That shiny new car will one day be a useless hunk of rusted junk; that beautiful big house will be torn down eventually; and, as sad as it is to consider, everyone we know and love is destined to die. Scientists assure us that the universe itself is doomed to extinction. The problem here is that if everything eventually ceases to exist, then nothing has ultimate meaning or value. In a billion trillion years, when the earth is gone and everyone who ever lived is forgotten, will anything you learned or accomplished or owned matter? As King Solomon, a man who had everything the world had to offer, realized, death sucks the purpose out of everything. He gained wisdom, but came to realize that, ultimately, the wise man is no better off than the fool:

> The same fate overtakes them both. Then I said to myself, "The fate of the fool will overtake me also. What then do I gain by being wise?" I said to myself, "This too is meaningless." For the wise man, like the fool, will not be long remembered; the days have already come when both will be forgotten. Like the fool, the wise too must die! So I hated life, because the work that is done under the sun was grievous to me. All of it is meaningless, a chasing after the wind.
>
> Ecclesiastes 2:14–17

William Lane Craig notes,

> If each individual person passes out of existence when he dies, then what ultimate meaning can be given to his life? Does it really matter whether he ever existed at all? It might be said that his life was important because it influenced others or affected the course of history. But this shows only a relative significance to his life, not an ultimate significance. His life may be important

194

relative to certain other events, but what is the ultimate significance of any of those events? If all the events are meaningless,
then what can be the ultimate significance of influencing any
of them? Ultimately it makes no difference.[13]

In other words, your environmental activism may have an effect on life here and now, but it will have no ultimate effect. The
end will be the same regardless of what anyone does. Craig's
Reasonable Faith, particularly chapter 2 on the absurdity of life
without God, is excellent in this area, and discussing this may
help the skeptic see your point about the insufficiency of worldly
goods to satisfy. However, as I said above, if he won't agree to
your data point fairly quickly, I suggest choosing another piece
of evidence to discuss. Assuming that most people will agree
with the idea that all people long for something more in life,
let's move on to explaining that fact.

Step Two: Offer the Christian Explanation of the Data

I've switched the order of steps for this chapter (putting the
Christian explanation ahead of the skeptic's) because the Christian is presenting the evidence and the conversation will probably flow naturally into the believer's explanation of that data.
However, as I mentioned in the last chapter, this is obviously
not a hard-and-fast rule. If the skeptic jumps in and offers her
explanation, and you want to discuss it first, of course that's fine.

A Desire for God

According to the Christian worldview, the reason nothing
on earth satisfies our deepest desire is that we do not desire
anything on earth. Rather, we desire God. More specifically,
we desire the intimate relationship with God for which we were

created and that we lost at the fall. Even more specifically, we long for true love. We are desperate to love and be loved by our heavenly Father. Because, as we saw in chapter 4, if we love ourselves and the creation more than the Creator we are unsatisfied. Disordered love creates chaos, not contentment. C. S. Lewis explains that when Satan convinced Adam and Eve that they could be their own gods, he was selling the idea that humans could create happiness for themselves apart from their creator. "And out of that hopeless attempt has come nearly all that we call human history—money, poverty, ambition, war, prostitution, [social] classes, empires, slavery—the long, terrible story of man trying to find something other than God which will make him happy."[14] This will never work because we were created *for* God: "God cannot give us happiness and peace apart from Himself, because it is not there. There is no such thing."[15]

As creatures designed for relationship with God, we cannot escape the fact that we will never be fulfilled until we have that relationship. Kreeft offers good insight in this area as well:

> Like it or not, we come into this world with predesigned equipment, spiritual as well as physical. And we can never alter or erase that design, no matter how desperately and darkly we try. We are cursed with the knowledge of God. We are spoiled by our knowledge of the Best and can therefore never be totally satisfied with anything less.[16]

This truth has been stated many ways over the centuries. Saint Augustine famously said that, even in his sinful and rebellious state, part of man longs to praise God. "The thought of you stirs him so deeply that he cannot be content unless he praises you, because you made us for yourself and our hearts find no peace until they rest in you."[17]

Randy Alcorn calls this a longing for heaven, the place where this rest will be complete:

> Nothing is more often misdiagnosed than our homesickness for Heaven. We think that what we want is sex, drugs, alcohol, a new job, a raise, a doctorate, a spouse, a large-screen television, a new car, a cabin in the woods, a condo in Hawaii. What we really want is the person we were made for, Jesus, and the place we were made for, Heaven. Nothing less can satisfy us.[18]

Kreeft makes the same argument in suggesting that what we really seek is *agape*, the love of God. He notes that, while the perfection of our relationship with God will occur in heaven, the relationship with God that we long for is available right now.

> The deeper and more honestly we look, the closer we approach Ecclesiastes' terrifying truth about this world: "Vanity of vanities, all is vanity." . . . Nothing here under the sun can fill our hearts and still our restlessness. But God can fill us and still us, and God is *agape*, and *agape* is here under the sun. *Agape* is eternal because it is the very stuff of God. That is why it is the only thing in life that never gets boring. Not ever. *Agape* is the only answer to Ecclesiastes. Ecclesiastes says, "I have seen everything" (Ecclesiastes 1:14). But he has not. He missed one thing: *agape*.[19]

So while we may never completely eradicate the longing we feel for heaven until we get there, part of our desires can be met by a current relationship with God.

Regardless of their various points of emphasis, these theologians all agree that the unfulfilled longing people feel is the result of being separated from God. Only God will fill the hole in our lives. In fact, God has erased the ache that millions of people have felt before they met him.

Here you could tell your own story of finding peace and contentment through a relationship with Jesus (assuming you have one and have found some peace) or relate the testimony of any of the millions of other Christians in history that have done the same. Take Saint Augustine, for example. His classic *Confessions* is all about how he struggled to discard his "load of vanity"[20]—all the earthly goods he had chased so hard after and yet failed to satisfy—and finally found fulfillment in Christ.

In my own case, I came to an abrupt realization of the futility of earthly goods while lying on a hospital bed completely unable to move. It was the early nineties, and I was a typical cocky young twenty-something, living for nothing more than a good time. My friend and I were driving home from playing hockey in southern Saskatchewan when my beloved black Chevy short-box hit a patch of black ice on a bridge and slid into a ditch filled with hard-packed snow. The truck flipped several times, throwing me out the driver's side window before coming to a rest just inches from my head. I woke up in the hospital, paralyzed. All I could think of was what a waste my life had been to that point. I had made some money and had some fun, but for what? Right then and there I told God he could do whatever he wanted to do with me. If that meant going to Africa as a missionary (the standard fear of every pious young evangelical I knew), well, so be it, but I was done chasing after stuff that would never satisfy.

It was a key turning point in my life. By the next morning I was able to move (there had been no major injuries) and I was released from the hospital later that day. I was also released from the confines of a meaningless and empty life. As I will talk about more in the next chapter, God has faithfully guided and supported me since that day, and I have never for a second regretted surrendering my life to him. He has brought me joy, contentment, and purpose beyond my wildest dreams.

A Possible Objection to the Christian Explanation

Let's briefly address a popular objection you might hear to the Christian explanation of longing: "The fact that we long for something doesn't mean that it exists. Even if I grant that we long for God, that doesn't prove that he exists. When I was young, I wished that Santa Claus was real, but that didn't make it so."

First, we are not trying to *prove* God exists in the mathematical sense. This is not a logical syllogism that states, "I long, therefore God must exist." We are practicing inference to the best explanation. We think the data of longing is best explained within the Christian worldview; that is not to say that other explanations are not possible.

Second, we need to make a distinction between innate natural desires and externally conditioned artificial desires. We naturally desire things like food, sleep, and friendship and naturally shun things like starvation and loneliness. On the other hand, we also may desire fame, fortune, and the ability to leap tall buildings in a single bound, but these do not come from within us. They are socially conditioned by advertising, TV, comic books, and the like. Natural desires are universal, but artificial desires vary from person to person. Also, we do not recognize the lack of an artificial desire in the same way we do a natural one. We commonly refer to being hungry or tired, but we don't think in terms such as "Ferrari-less."[21] All this to say that natural desires always correspond to things that exist. As C. S. Lewis reasoned,

> A baby feels hunger: well, there is such a thing as food. A duckling wants to swim: well, there is such a thing as water. Man feels sexual desire: well, there is such a thing as sex. If I find in myself a desire which no experience in this world can satisfy, the most probable explanation is that I was made for another world.[22]

This doesn't mean that we always attain the objects of our desires. However, it is a good indication that the objects exist.

> A man's physical hunger does not prove that man will get any bread; he may die of starvation on a raft in the Atlantic. But surely a man's hunger does prove that he comes of a race which repairs its body by eating and inhabits a world where eatable substances exist. In the same way, though I do not believe (I wish I did) that my desire for Paradise proves that I shall enjoy it, I think it a pretty good indication that such a thing exists and that some men will.[23]

Step Three: Evaluate Alternate Explanations

Frankly, I'm not sure what you will hear in the way of alternate explanations for longing. In my experience, skeptics, if they can come up with anything at all, are all over the map on this one. However, that is not to say that there are no alternate answers. Thinkers have been trying to come up with a solution to the problem of discontentment since the fall. Indeed, that quest has been at least partly responsible for some of the more serious and enduring philosophies and religions in the history of the world. It's just that these ideas have not really taken hold in common American consciousness. That said, I do want to address, in broad strokes and on a very popular level, three theories that you may run into (in one form or another) in day-to-day conversation. We'll start with the one that developed most recently and move our way backward in history.

The Existentialist Answer

The most common response you hear will probably sound something like this: "Well, okay, maybe there is nothing outside of us that will satisfy everyone's longing, but I just think it's up to each of us individually to choose our own meaning in life. We can be fulfilled; we just have to decide for ourselves *how* we want to be fulfilled."

This response owes much to nineteenth- and twentieth-century atheist existentialist philosophers like as Jean-Paul Sartre. After coming to the realization that life without God is absurd and objectively pointless, Sartre was filled with anguish, abandonment, and despair at the prospect of facing a world in which he was without a transcendent guide or purpose.[24] He posited that man must create purpose for himself by following a freely chosen path. Sartre settled on Marxism.

You see this mind-set in the current preoccupation of our youth in finding something to join that is "bigger than themselves." From communism to environmentalism, people sign on because it provides them something to live for beyond their paycheck. Al Gore made this point explicit in a *New York Times* op-ed about why everyone should be a part of his anti-global-warming crusade. After explaining that there would be some financial benefits from a switch to clean energy, he concludes:

> But there's something even more precious to be gained if we do the right thing. The climate crisis offers us the chance to experience what few generations in history have had the privilege of experiencing: a generational mission; a compelling moral purpose; a shared cause; and the thrill of being forced by circumstances to put aside the pettiness and conflict of politics and to embrace a genuine moral and spiritual challenge.[25]

This is an existentialist statement. Gore is saying that, contrary to what previous generations of unfortunate fools had done, this generation can find a meaning in life by choosing to join the anti-global-warming movement.

The obvious flaw in this thinking is that the whole notion of self-created meaning is absurd on its face. As Craig points out:

> Without God, there can be no objective meaning in life. Sartre's program is actually an exercise in self-delusion. For the universe does not really acquire meaning just because *I* happen to give it one. This is easy to see: for suppose I give the universe one meaning, and you give it another. Who is right? The answer, of course, is neither one. For the universe without God remains objectively meaningless, no matter how *we* regard it. Sartre is really saying, "Let's *pretend* the universe has meaning." And this is just fooling ourselves.[26]

Also, what if the "meaning" you choose for your life is evil? Sartre chose Marxism, an ideology that presided over more than 100 million murders in the twentieth century. Was that a valid choice? This is something you might ask the person who thinks we should choose our own meaning in life. If there is no ultimate standard, is finding "fulfillment" by breaking into homes and stealing your neighbor's stuff okay? These are the kinds of logical ramifications you will want to explore with an existentialist.

The Stoic Answer

The Stoic agrees with the existentialist that we need to tackle the problem of longing by exercising our will. However, where the existentialist claims we should choose to find fulfillment in something, the Stoic says we should choose to stop desiring fulfillment at all.

Stoicism began about 300 BC and is represented in the thought of philosophers such as Marcus Aurelius and Epictetus. They taught that almost all types of human desire are subordinate to the will. In other words, if you feel a need for something, it is because you chose to feel that need, or at least allowed yourself to feel it. Feelings don't occur unless you exercise your will. As Epictetus wrote, "If, therefore, any be unhappy, let him remember that he is unhappy by reason of himself alone."[27] In other words, if you are sad, it's not because of outward circumstances, it's your own fault for choosing to be sad. Consequently, they reasoned, the key to getting rid of longing is to simply choose to stop longing.

While it is certainly true that our choices can influence and direct our feelings for good or ill, the Stoic view goes too far in attempting to deny our natural desires and emotional responses to objective reality. For example, it is perfectly normal to be sad when a loved one dies. To attempt, through an act of will, not to be sad is to act contrary to our true nature. There may be a time to "suck it up," but at a certain point that becomes destructive.[28] It is like trying not to be hungry after not eating for a few days. While willpower can have positive effects on our appetite, at some point the body legitimately needs food, and to suppress that desire is actually harmful.

As I mentioned earlier, there is a difference between natural longings, such as hunger, and artificial longings, such as the desire for a Ferrari. Natural longings are not fundamentally the result of choice. While it might be right to stop longing for a sports car, one should not stop wanting to eat, although we may want to stop wanting to eat quite as much as we do. Existential angst is a natural desire that needs to find its object. We need God, and no amount of willpower will change that.

Eastern Answers

Buddhism and Hinduism, currently in vogue among many Westerners, are both directly concerned with humanity's discontentment and have similar prescriptions to the problem of desire.

For example, "The Four Noble Truths" of Buddhism (arguably the central teaching of that religion) address the problem of humanity's unfulfilled longing explicitly. The first truth is that life lacks satisfaction. While people may find happiness for a moment here and there, it is always fleeting. Everything changes and so nothing keeps us content. The second truth is that we are dissatisfied because we crave and cling and thirst. We need to get rid of that desire, which is the result of ignorance. The problem is that we see a distinction between ourselves and the thing we desire. We think that the things of the world will add something to our lives if we could only attach ourselves to them. In reality, according to Buddhism, there is no separation between you and things. All is one. To desire something is to mistakenly think that you exist independently from the thing you desire. The third and fourth truths teach how to reach a level of experience in which you "realize emptiness" and cease to desire anything, largely because there ceases to be a "you" to do anything at all. All distinctions are gone.

Hinduism, for its part, similarly teaches that the goal of its various paths and stages of life is "liberation" from the desires of life and union with the divine. Although it recognizes that people can legitimately give themselves to lesser goals, such as sensual pleasure, wealth, worldly success, and moral duty, ultimately the goal is to escape worldly pursuits and the worldly cycle of death and rebirth to enter Nirvana, where these desires will be no more.

In discussing and evaluating these positions, I usually emphasize the logical ramifications of the teaching that all distinctions are illusions. If everything is actually one, not only are you not different from the thing you desire, you are no different than me or that tree over there. Personhood is an illusion. Does this seem like the best explanation of the evidence? No one lives as if that is true. Also, this teaching means that there is no such thing as good or evil, as those distinctions are illusory as well. Is your conversation partner willing to admit that the difference between Hitler and Mother Teresa is ultimately an illusion? Not likely. And if they do, that just helps you clarify further the difference between Christianity and Eastern belief systems: Whereas those worldviews explain away a plain sense interpretation of our most basic experiences (i.e., being different from a rock, judging Hitler as evil) as illusions, Christianity accepts them as valid and correct.

Conclusion

In answer to the problem of longing, the Christian worldview is the only one that treats our desire for transcendence as real. It teaches that those longings correspond to something or someone outside of ourselves and can be fulfilled by finding relationship with God. In other words, Christianity treats our longing for God as if it were the same as longing for water and food. If you want to be satisfied, eat and drink. Let's revisit the famous passage from Isaiah:

> Come, all you who are thirsty, come to the waters; and you who have no money, come, buy and eat! Come, buy wine and milk without money and without cost. Why spend money on what is not bread, and your labor on what does not satisfy? Listen, listen to me, and eat what is good, and you will delight in the richest of fare. Give ear and come to me; listen, that you may live.
>
> 55:1–3

On the other hand, all the other views we mentioned (and many others we didn't) focus on the desire itself as the problem. The existentialist says that we must change our desire, settling for something less than what we thought we needed. The Stoic says we must get rid of our desire. And the Buddhist or Hindu pantheist says we have to realize that there is nothing to desire. In other words, if they were talking about one's desire for food, they would say: Try to live on air instead of food, stop wanting food, or realize that food is an illusion. What makes the most sense of the data?

Up Close and Personal
With God

"But What About Edwina?"

One of my favorite children's books of all time is called *Edwina: The Dinosaur Who Didn't Know She Was Extinct*. Written and illustrated by the marvelously talented Mo Willems, *Edwina* is the story of a very good and kind dinosaur. She plays with the kids, helps little old ladies cross the street, and, best of all, bakes delicious chocolate chip cookies to give away. Everyone loves Edwina. Everyone, that is, except young Reginald Von Hoobie-Doobie. Along with having the best name in all of children's literature, Reginald is the town know-it-all, and he is on a mission to convince everyone that dinosaurs are extinct. To accomplish this he gives speeches, hands out flyers, and even stages protests in the streets. The funniest picture in the book is of Reginald holding a handmade sign while standing in front of Edwina buying an ice-cream cone for a little girl. The sign reads: THIS IS NOT HAPPENING.

In another scene, Reginald lectures his classmates about just how totally extinct dinosaurs really are. But as soon as he begins to speak, the kids start asking questions. Beth McFeeder pipes up: "'What about Edwina? She's a dinosaur.' Then Tommy Britcher says, 'Yeah, Edwina can't be extinct. She bakes chocolate chip cookies for us!'"[1] Even the teacher gets in on the act, suggesting that Edwina might be making cookies for them right at that moment. At this, the class empties to go find some cookies, leaving Reginald with his notes.

I can relate to those students. Every time I read *Edwina*, Reginald Von Hoobie-Doobie reminds me of a typical religious skeptic. That is not to say that believing in God is like believing in the current existence of dinosaurs, of course, but Reginald's attitude of staunch disbelief in the face of clear evidence, particularly the evidence of personal experience, is strikingly similar to that of most skeptics I talk to. Frankly, I often find myself thinking, *I appreciate your earnestness, and I understand that you think you have a really good argument, but seriously, you are trying to convince me that God doesn't exist? After all we have been through together, and after he has been so good to me? Good luck with that.*

Seemingly Strong Evidence That Is Rarely Shared

When it comes to supporting a Christian worldview, the evidence of personal experience is somewhat of a paradox. On one hand, most of the people I know who have a very strong faith seem to base that trust largely on what they consider to be divine intervention in their lives and direct personal encounters with God. They point to answered prayer, mystical experiences, miraculous healing, and providential guidance as the key events in their lives. While they usually have many other good reasons for belief as well, ultimately it is their personal experience that provides the foundation of their faith. It seems that experience plays a major role in convincing people that God is real and ensuring them that he is good.

Sociologist Christian Smith supports my thesis. After conducting a wide-ranging study of American believers, he concluded, "Very many modern people have encountered and do encounter what are to them very real spiritual experiences, frequently vivid and powerful ones. And these often serve as epistemological anchors sustaining their religious faith in even the most pluralistic and secular of situations."[2] Even in a culture full of Reginald Von Hoobie-Doobies telling us that God doesn't exist, people keep on believing because they know him experientially.

On the other hand, these encounters with God are rarely used in evangelism or apologetics. They may be considered, on a personal level, the most solid piece of evidence one has for belief, but they seldom get entered into a discussion as data that skeptics might also want to consider. Indeed, they are often not even shared among fellow believers as a way of strengthening one another's faith.

For example, J. P. Moreland tells the story of an episode that took place while he was speaking at a large church about how to nurture confidence in God. During a coffee break, a member of the ministry staff told Moreland about how he had been miraculously healed several years before. The young man's chest and hands had been fractured in an accident at a machine shop. At the hospital, he was X-rayed and told to return the next morning for more tests.

That evening, some Christian friends came to his house and prayed for his healing. Even though he was on pain medication, he could still feel pain; however, as the people prayed, the pain vanished and the swelling in his hands left. He was startled. The next morning, the surgeons took new X-rays, which indicated that the fractures were completely healed. The doctors also noted that the swelling was gone, something that just does not happen so quickly on its own. When the doctors compared the two sets of X-rays, it was clear that he had been miraculously healed! The fracture lines were gone![3]

Interestingly, when Moreland asked the man if he had ever told anyone about this story, the answer was no. "He didn't want to talk about himself or appear weird to people."[4]

This is consistent with my findings as well. Apologists, evangelists, and other ministers of the gospel often have very strong personal testimonies of God's intervention in their lives, but they very rarely share them with others. There are several reasons for this. We'll start with the two mentioned in the story.

Humility

The young church staff member didn't want to gloat over his miraculous healing, and of course that's the right attitude. We are not to glory in ourselves, as if our own righteousness or skill was responsible for a supernatural occurrence. However, that does not mean that we shouldn't celebrate what God has done and share it with others. Indeed, remembering and celebrating God's action is an important spiritual discipline for fostering greater trust in him. God filled the Israelite calendar with festivals and feasts for this very reason.

Proclaiming these acts is also an important part of reaching others. For example, in the first evangelistic sermon Peter ever preached (in the midst of an outpouring of supernatural signs and wonders at Pentecost), he emphasized the evidence of the miraculous: "Fellow Israelites, listen to this: Jesus of Nazareth was a man accredited by God to you by miracles, wonders and signs, which God did among you through him, as you yourselves know" (Acts 2:22). Also, Paul consistently shared the story of his vision on the road to Damascus (e.g., Acts 22 and 26). Spiritual experiences can theoretically cause a person to be conceited (see 2 Corinthians 12:7), but guarding against pride does not necessitate that we keep silent about all that God has done.

The Weirdness Factor

I don't know exactly what the young man was thinking in not wanting to be considered "weird," but I suspect he didn't want to be associated with charlatans. Again, this is understandable. Nobody wants to be lumped in with crooked "faith healers" and televangelists who make all sorts of fraudulent claims. However, the fact that counterfeits exist does not mean that the real thing does not. We can't stop telling true stories just because other people tell false ones.

Playing by the Skeptic's Rules

The desire not to appear "weird" may also be a sign of something more problematic: an implicit acceptance of many of our society's secularist and naturalistic assumptions about life. As Clint Arnold has suggested, "Many Western Christians have adopted elements of an anti-supernatural bias, perhaps even unwittingly, through the influence of our prevailing culture."[5]

One of the places this bias shows up is in our belief regarding what may reasonably be discussed in the public square. For generations we have been told that religious experiences are private matters that should be kept private. If you want to talk

211

about them in your prayer meetings and church services, that's fine, but don't bring them outside those walls. The underlying idea here is that religious experiences don't offer us any objective information about reality anyway.[6]

This is false, and we need to be very careful about implicitly accepting that lie by refusing to offer spiritual experiences as evidence in a worldview discussion. In doing so we are essentially playing by the skeptic's rules; we are submitting to an argument format that presupposes there is no God in order to try to argue that he exists.

We also see this attitude in the reluctance of Christians to speak about apparent encounters with supernatural beings, a hesitancy to which I plead guilty as well.

In the 1990s, I spent several years working at a camp for inner-city youth. One night I got a call to come help with a rowdy boy who was causing trouble. When I arrived at the dining hall, I could see that this was no ordinary case. The boy was screaming, attacking people, and tearing the place up with a strength and zeal that just didn't seem to fit his body. I finally got my arms around him in a bear hug, but it was all I could do to keep him from injuring me and the others around him. As he continued to flail and yell, the camp director, Heather, and I were at a loss as to what to do. The boy didn't seem to be tiring out, but I certainly was. Heather decided to pray. I don't remember what words she used, exactly, but I vividly remember what happened the millisecond she said "Amen": The boy fell asleep. I mean, instantly. He was completely out, with his head resting on my shoulder. He went from cussing and punching to unconscious in the blink of an eye. We were shocked. I carried the boy down to the nurses' station and put him to bed. Several hours later he awoke with a smile, laughing and joking. He seemed to be a brand-new person.

Now, none of us on staff had a particularly charismatic background. We were not ones to see angels and demons under every stone. However, we all came to the same conclusion about our experience that night: Supernatural forces were at work.

As I said, people are not usually forthcoming with these kinds of stories. I think I've talked about this episode about twice in the fifteen years since it happened. However, interaction with the spiritual world is a much more common and widespread phenomenon than is usually acknowledged. If you ask around, I'll bet you'd be surprised at how many people will have an experience to share. An article in the alumni newsletter of Biola University (hardly a bastion of wild-eyed demon-fighters) offers a good example. Holly Pivec interviewed six PhD-holding professors, all of whom believed they had witnessed demonic phenomena, from flying objects to supernatural knowledge.[7] Moreland and Issler, also Biola professors (although neither was mentioned in the article), sum up my thoughts exactly: "We know many credible, honest people who have encountered angels and demons in various circumstances. The combined weight of their testimony has brought both of us to the point that we simply cannot doubt the reality of angels and demons even if we wanted to."[8] And why would we want to, anyway? The existence of angels and demons is clearly scriptural. We shouldn't be shy about sharing these experiences as evidence just because the materialistic culture scoffs at them.[9]

Inherently Unreliable?

Another reason that Christians don't share spiritual experiences is that they believe personal testimonies are inherently unreliable. Many people seem to think, "If it's just my word, what good is that?" Well, assuming you are honest, it's plenty

213

good. The fact is, unless there are some valid reasons not to, we accept the testimony of others all the time. In general, we give people the benefit of the doubt. We don't assume someone has been deceived or is lying. He might be, but as Groothuis notes: "The burden of proof lies on establishing guilt, not in establishing innocence."[10]

Of course, some stories are better supported than others and therefore are more believable. For example, I suggest that if you use a story from your own life when talking to skeptics, it should be one that can be easily verified by others who were present.[11] Also, in choosing which stories to recount (whether your own story or someone else's), you should follow the principle of the *credible witness*. As Moreland explains, "A credible witness is someone we trust who is stable, reliable and informed enough to be qualified to testify to something, who has no reason to lie or exaggerate, and who is respected in the broader Christian community or among those whom you know well."[12]

Too Subjective?

Another common reason for not sharing our personal stories is that the whole realm of spiritual experiences seems too subjective. We all know the door-to-door missionaries who support their truth claims by asking the potential convert to "pray about it" or by appealing to a personal experience (i.e., a "burning in the bosom") that is supposed to validate their message. I once asked a couple of young Mormon elders why they believed their teaching to be true. They told me about how they had each gone on a mountain retreat before heading out on their mission. At one point during their stay they were sent into the woods in order to seek a "Joseph Smith experience" that would confirm for them that their religion was true and that they were called to proclaim its message. When I asked them whether or not they had had such an experience and if they could describe it, both struggled to answer before essentially refusing to comment any further. From what I could gather, either they didn't have the same experience, didn't have an experience they could describe, or didn't have an experience at all. It was all very vague.

This kind of approach didn't go far with me and won't go far with a skeptic. It is simply too subjective to discuss. There is no way to evaluate what kind of experience, if any, the missionaries had, or whether their interpretation of it was accurate. As evidence, a self-authenticating experience such as this just isn't effective in evangelism and apologetics. I don't know if those guys were indicative of all LDS members or if they were in line with the official teaching of that church, but the fact that they couldn't offer any evidence (historical, philosophical, archaeological, etc.) other than subjective experience to support their religious views was a huge problem.

However, orthodox Christianity does not have that difficulty. For one thing, Christianity does not rely solely on experience to support its truth claims. As we have seen, there are all kinds of different types of evidence for the Christian worldview. As a result, the personal experiences that Christianity presents as evidence are not self-authenticating. They are dependent on those other types of evidence for support and interpretation.

For example, if God reveals himself through nature and Scripture, then I can't interpret my experience to contradict the truth found in these other places. I've heard of several pastors who left their wives and ran off with the church secretary after claiming they heard a "voice" from God telling them it was okay. From the perspective of a Christian worldview, this is ridiculous. As Blackaby rightly points out, subjective experience alone cannot be your guide.

At times as I'm leading a seminar, someone will get upset with me and say, "Well, I don't care what you say; I've experienced such and such." I respond as kindly as I know how by saying, "I do not deny your experience. I do question your interpretation of what you experienced because it is contrary to what I see in the Word of God." . . . Every experience must be held up against the Scriptures.[13]

Also, Christian experiences should be held up against the long tradition of the church. In order for an experience to have evidential power in a discussion, it should have been experienced by many others before you. As Michael Novak writes:

> The experiences of Christians are not always merely "subjective." Sometimes they *are*, and such opinions are likely to be brushed aside by others. But sometimes certain experiences awaken memories of yet others, well recognized in a long tradition. Sometimes, personal experiences meet other criteria that lift them from the merely "subjective" into what might be called the "intersubjective."[14]

For example, many times in my life I have opened up the Bible "at random" and the first words I read seemed to be God saying exactly what I needed to hear at that very moment. In one instance I remember vividly, I was feeling particularly discouraged. My ministry was not "taking off" the way I had hoped, and my seemingly endless graduate studies were putting a financial strain on my family. While most of my peers were buying houses and getting well established in their careers, I was struggling to get by on student loans and low-paying jobs. I was seriously considering throwing in the towel and going to find a "real" life. I slumped in my chair and let my Bible fall open. I read the first passage I saw:

> Apply your heart to instruction and your ears to words of knowledge. . . . My son, if your heart is wise, then my heart will be

glad indeed; my inmost being will rejoice when your lips speak what is right. Do not let your heart envy sinners, but always be zealous for the fear of the LORD. There is surely a future hope for you, and your hope will not be cut off.

Proverbs 23:12, 15–18

I can't tell you how encouraged I was in reading that (or how many times I have returned to meditate on that passage over the years).

Now, you might say that I just got lucky, or that this is not proper biblical hermeneutics. Doesn't this kind of approach to Scripture contradict what I said in chapter 8? I don't think so. For one, my understanding of what God said to me does not contradict the literal or spiritual sense of that text. Also, and this is the main point I am making in this section, there is a long tradition in the church of God speaking to people in just this way. I personally know many people who have had this experience, and it goes back to the beginnings of the church. Let's return to the story of Augustine's conversion for a good example.

Augustine had been wrestling with God a long time, but had been unable to break free from the "sordid and shameful" habits of his youth and surrender his life to God. However, one day, while crying out to God in a garden in Milan, Augustine heard the voice nearby of a child singing over and over again the words "Take it and read." As he recounts in his *Confessions*, Augustine took this as a

> divine command to open my book of Scripture and read the first passage on which my eyes should fall. For I had heard the story of Antony, and I remembered how he had happened to go into a church while the Gospel was being read and had taken it as a counsel addressed to himself when he heard the words *Go home and sell all that belongs to you. Give it to the poor, and*

so the treasure you have shall be in heaven; then come back and follow me [Matthew 19:21]. By this divine pronouncement, he had at once been converted to you.

So I hurried back . . . opened [the Bible], and in silence I read the first passage on which my eyes fell: *Not in revelling and drunkenness, not in lust and wantonness, not in quarrels and rivalries. Rather, arm yourselves with the Lord Jesus Christ; spend no more thought on nature and nature's appetites* [Romans 13:13–14]. I had no wish to read more and no need to do so. For in an instant, as I came to the end of the sentence, it was as though the light of confidence flooded into my heart and all the darkness of doubt was dispelled.[15]

Notice that not only did Augustine have a similar experience to me, but the same thing had already happened to Antony. This is the type of "cross-referencing" that needs to be characteristic of experiential data.

We can also judge experiences by the objectively measurable results they produce. For example, one of the more famous "personal religious experiences" in the New Testament is Saul's meeting with the risen Jesus on the road to Damascus (Acts 9). After Saul saw light from heaven and heard a voice telling him what to do, he turned from being a persecutor of believers to the world's greatest missionary. Several aspects of the story make Saul's experience more than just subjective. First, although the men traveling with Saul did not see Jesus, they heard something and clearly shared in his experience enough to be shocked by it (Acts 9:7). They could testify that Saul wasn't just making stuff up. Second, they could see the change that came over Saul. This character transformation is part of the data that must be accounted for. The fact that millions of people over the years have been changed in a similar way to Saul after claiming to meet Jesus, and that these experiences were predicted in the

Old Testament (e.g., Ezekiel 36:26), takes these experiences even further away from the realm of the completely subjective.

Let's move on to apply these principles to a few specific examples as we walk through our usual discussion steps.

Step One: Present the Data

As we've already seen, there are many different types of experiences you can present as data. Frankly, I struggled to decide what experiences to focus on in this section. For one thing, there are literally millions of testimonials available to choose from, many of them highly trustworthy and extraordinarily moving. How could I whittle it down to just a few? Also, what types of experiences should I focus on? We've already talked about, albeit far too briefly, seemingly miraculous healings,[16] encounters with supernatural forces, and divine communication. I could also speak about the mystical presence of God as experienced by the great saints,[17] dead children being raised to life in India,[18] or the visions of Jesus occurring by the thousands among Muslims in the Middle East.[19] These all have tremendous value as evidence for the Christian worldview.

In the end I decided to go with some experiences that might seem less sensational, but are more in line with how most of us experience God in everyday life. They primarily have to do with "personal providence": the sense that someone powerful is watching over us and directing events for our good. These examples may not have the Wow! factor of some other experiences, but they are still solid pieces of evidence for the Christian worldview. They also have the benefit of coming across as highly authentic and verifiable.

I suggest that you share your own similar experiences or those of family or close friends. You will be sharing your own life. Hence, I think you will have an easier time getting the skeptic to (1) believe the experiences happened and (2) relate them to something he may actually experience (or has already experienced) himself.

Divine Protection

My wife and I enjoy *Deadliest Catch*, a reality TV show about a bunch of Bering Sea crab fishermen, some of the toughest guys on the planet. On a recent episode, Edgar Hansen, deck boss of the *Northwestern*, sensed that something was wrong with the boat. On a "whim," he opened up a hatch on deck to find one of the compartments taking on water and almost full. A warning sensor that would have alerted the crew to this problem was broken. If they had continued working only a few more minutes, the ship would have become unstable and potentially sunk. Because Edgar found it when he did, they were able to pump out the water and save the ship. What I found interesting was the way the crew reacted. "Someone is watching over us," Captain Sig Hansen asserted, and Edgar himself gave a hearty thank-you to God (or whoever he was thinking of as he looked to the sky) for keeping them safe.[20]

I've spoken the same words thousands of times in my life. It's what I said when I heard how close my truck had come to crushing me, and it's what I say almost every day while traveling the Southern California freeways I use to get to my office. Millions of people have had a sense that God (perhaps through angels) is working to keep us safe. Sometimes this takes more flamboyant forms (like the mother trapped in the Joplin, Missouri, tornado who felt an angelic "force" protecting her and her daughters from shards of glass[21]), but most of us interpret even the more mundane variety as instances of divine protection.

220

Divine Provision

Just a few moments ago, as I prepared to write this section of the chapter, the man from the office next to mine stopped by for a quick chat. Somehow the discussion turned to retirement plans and he asked me if I had one. "Sure," I explained with a smile, "God is my retirement plan." By that I meant that God had been incredibly faithful in providing for my needs thus far in my life, and I expected him to continue to do that until I died. My friend then launched into a story about his brother the missionary. I won't go into all the details here, but the bottom line of the story was that at several points in his ministry the brother had found himself in a tight financial pinch. At every juncture along the way, money had "turned up" from an unexpected source, sometimes in exactly the amount needed.

That has been my experience as well. Indeed, the instances in my life that I consider to be divine provision are way too numerous to remember, let alone recount here. I'll just offer one that is typical: About a year after launching Don Johnson Ministries, we started purchasing airtime to do a radio show in the Los Angeles area. It was a big investment for us, considering our support base was not very large, but we stepped out in faith. After about four months, it looked like we were going to have to take a step back. We simply didn't have the funds to keep the show on the air, so on a Friday we decided that on Monday we would call the station and cancel the program. However, on that Saturday an anonymous check came in the mail for $10,000. It was by far the biggest donation we had ever received, and to this day I don't know who sent it. I know who to thank for it, though.

This type of experience is really quite commonplace. There are several trustworthy sources for more stories like this one, including *In Search of a Confident Faith* by J. P. Moreland and Klaus Issler.

Divine Control Over Events

In the spring of 2008, I went with a team of evangelists to hold outreach festivals in various towns and villages in southern India. Almost from the time I touched down, I was repeatedly warned about one of the locations to which I had been assigned. "You must be very careful about what you preach there," several people said. "The political leaders in that area want nothing to do with Christianity. They are glad to have an American coming to town to put on a show, but they don't want to hear about Jesus being the only way of salvation, or anything like that. If you speak in that way, there may be serious consequences. Please just give a more generic message that won't offend anyone."

This presented a dilemma, obviously, as I don't run an evangelistic ministry and set up events halfway around the world in order *not* to preach the gospel. So we prayed about it and determined that I would just have to proclaim my usual message and let the chips fall where they may. In the back of my mind I hoped that perhaps word would not get back to the politicians before we finished the outreach and got back on the plane.

That dream quickly vanished when we arrived for the festival. There on the stage were all the dignitaries and political leaders of the region, including the man we had been warned about most. He had made a special trip to attend this event and would be saying a few words before I preached. My heart raced all through the singing time and leader's speech (none of which I could understand), and as he finished up, I gathered my Bible and my notes and offered up one more quick prayer. Then a strange thing happened: The politician and his entire entourage left the stage and walked toward their cars. I quickly asked a local pastor what was happening. He explained that they had another meeting to get to in a distant city and would not be able to stay to hear me preach. What a relief! I praised God under my breath and went on with my message. The people responded very well, and at the end many came forward to talk to counselors about Jesus. However, that wasn't even the end of the story. As I drove back to my friend's house after the festival, he filled me in on the rest of the politician's remarks. Before he left, the man had explained to the crowd that it was a very special night because Jesus was present with them. He encouraged the people to listen very carefully to me so that they could learn how to know Jesus.

It was an amazing experience, but it was hardly unique. We live in a world in which somebody powerful seems to be guiding events, and many of us experience this sense of providence regularly.

Step Two: Offer the Christian Explanation of the Data

This one is fairly straightforward. The Christian position regarding experiences of personal providence is that God is active in the world today, working for the good of his people. This is the clear teaching of the Bible from start to finish, and, with the possible exception of some groups that believe God stopped doing signs and wonders after the early church got established, is basic Christian doctrine. Indeed, for Christians in most of the world, the idea of a Christian life that doesn't involve personal encounters with God and the supernatural realm would be considered so ridiculous as to be laughable.

Possible Objections

The main objection to this interpretation is almost inevitably going to be some variation of the "problem of evil": If God can protect and provide food and direct history for good, why do people die of cancer? Why do thousands of children starve to death every year? Why do tsunamis and earthquakes devastate

223

entire regions and wipe out so many innocent lives? Shouldn't God do something for those people too?

These are emotionally charged and serious questions, so they can't be ignored. However, they apply to the topic at hand only indirectly, so you need to be careful not to get sidetracked into changing the subject.

To illustrate, let's imagine we are first-century fishermen living by the Sea of Galilee. One day, after tying up our boats, we run into an excited crowd of people who claim to have been miraculously fed by Jesus. "He turned five loaves and two small fish into a feast for five thousand people!" they exclaim as they rush around the lake in search of another free meal. Then we meet a couple of his disciples who claim that he calmed a storm and kept them from drowning. "Interesting!" you say to me, "I wonder if the stories are true. Let's go check it out." But I am not interested: "If there is a miracle worker in the region, why didn't we get any food? And why didn't this Jesus show up and save my uncle from drowning in this godforsaken lake last month? These stories are clearly false. I don't think the guy even exists."

I hope you can see the logical fallacy here. It does not follow that just because Jesus didn't do a miracle for me, he did not do a miracle for anyone. Jesus could protect and provide food for some people and not others; there is no law of the universe that says if some people are protected and fed, all must be fed. So it is perfectly reasonable, should the evidence support it, to believe that Jesus exists and did a miracle for some people and not for others.

In the same way, one can reasonably accept that God exists and is active in the world while also accepting that he does not always perform the same acts on behalf of everyone. The problem of evil actually has no bearing on whether God exists or whether he interacts with his creation in acts of personal providence. As James Spiegel notes, even if the objection about evil were relevant, "it only undermines certain beliefs about the *nature* of God." It does not disprove the existence of God. "At most, evil should prompt us to reconsider what *kind* of God exists, not *whether* God exists. To give up belief in a world creator because of the existence of evil is a blatant *non sequitur.*"[22]

Again, this is not to say that the problem of evil should be ignored, and we must be careful not to let "cold" logic override empathy and compassion for a skeptic who may be genuinely hurting and confused about why God didn't act in a particular situation. It's good and necessary to explore the issue of suffering. However, if you address the problem of evil, you should make it another topic for discussion rather than let it distract from the topic at hand, which is alleged personal experiences of the supernatural. You could say something like this: "I'd be glad to talk about why God allows bad things to happen,[23] and if you would like to switch to that subject, I'm happy to explain the Christian teaching on it as well as why I think the Christian worldview has a much better explanation for the existence of pain, suffering, and evil than any other worldview. However, right now we are trying to explain the fact that people perceive a divine hand orchestrating the world to some degree, and I would prefer to finish that topic first."

Of course, this only applies if you think the skeptic is presenting the problem of evil as a strictly academic objection to the Christian worldview. If he is speaking from a heartfelt need to figure out why God allowed something bad to happen in his life, then you probably want to switch to that topic right away.

Step Three: Discuss Alternate Explanations of the Data

As usual, it is impossible to predict exactly what theories you might get from skeptics to explain experiences of apparent personal providence. However, I think there are essentially only two positions. If the God of the Bible isn't at work in the world than either (1) some other deity is directing events or (2) nothing is.

Let's deal with option 1 first. The idea here is that experiences of personal providence might suggest a higher power, but they do not necessarily point to the God of the Bible. The author of our experiences could be the god of a different religion or some vague force that governs all. Maybe "fate" provided the money to keep the radio show on the air or perhaps Zeus sent an invisible thunder bolt that kept my truck from rolling over my head.

Certainly it is true that the experiences recounted in this chapter are not stand-alone, airtight proofs for the biblical worldview. In other words, if they were the only source of religious knowledge we had, they wouldn't get us to Christianity. But they are not all we have, and I have never claimed that they are sufficient to get us to Christianity. Rather, they are one piece of data that fits well with many other pieces to build a strong cumulative case for the biblical worldview.

As William Alston points out, though no one strand of Christian evidence may be completely sufficient to keep the faith secure, "when combined into a rope they all together have enough strength to do the job."[24] He notes that one's putative experience of God can be supported by appealing to

> the witness of others who are more advanced in the Christian life, to the revelation of God in His historical acts, and to general philosophical reasons for believing that God as construed in Christianity does exist and rules His creation.

These sources combine to provide a believer with reasons

> to suppose that there is a being of the sort she takes herself to be aware of in her Christian life, a being that could be expected to do the things she is aware of this being as doing. Conversely, when

these more indirect (at least more indirect from her perspective) sources seem dubious, seem to provide at best a tenuous and shaky indication of the reality in question, she can fall back on her immediate, intimate sense of the presence and activity of God in her life to (rightfully) assure herself that it is not all the work of human imagination.[25]

So we interpret our experiences in light of truths that we have gleaned from other sources, and our experiences, in turn, support the trustworthiness of those sources. I have many good non-experiential reasons to believe the God of the Bible exists, but no similar reasons to believe Zeus does. Ascribing protective power to Zeus based only on my experience would be unreasonable, in the same way as ascribing protective power to Jesus would be unreasonable if I had only my experience. But I have more than that. Therefore, I am much more justified in positing that the Christian God is behind my experiences of personal providence than I would be in suggesting it was another supernatural force. (This would include more mainstream deities, of course, although I won't take the time to go into a comparative analysis of world religions here.)

Option 2 is the preferred choice of most skeptics that I run into. A typical response generally goes something like this: "You might think there is some power guiding history and breaking into the natural world to help people, but there just isn't. You think you saw a miracle, but you didn't. You think God is watching over you, but he isn't. You got lucky, that's it."

Here is the bottom line: No matter how extraordinary your evidence, the skeptic (at least of the normal materialistic variety) will simply deny that your experience was supernatural.

These kinds of skeptics will never admit that an experience should be interpreted supernaturally. However, it is very important to note that this is not due to a reasoned evaluation of the evidence, but rather an *a priori* rejection of the very possibility of the supernatural. They start with the premise that God doesn't exist and reason from there that nothing could possibly be responsible for directing our circumstances. The presuppositions of the materialist regarding the nature of reality and how we gather knowledge preclude him from ever seeing God in day-to-day events.

To be more accurate, it's not that he will never see God, it's that he is forced to conclude that apparent (and what many would consider to be obvious) acts of divine providence are actually just all fluke coincidences. This is not an easy thing to do. Trying to interpret all of life materialistically is a continual fight against our intuitive sense of the meaning of common situations. As atheist extraordinaire Friedrich Nietzsche admitted in an illuminating passage called "Personal Providence," denying the reality of a divinely authored personal providence is a struggle:

> There is a certain high point in life; once we have reached it, we are, for all our freedom, once more in the greatest danger of spiritual unfreedom, and no matter how much we have confronted the beautiful chaos of existence and denied it all providential reason and goodness, we still have to pass our hardest test. For it is only now that the thought of a personal providence confronts us with the most penetrating force and the best advocate, appearance, speaks for it—now that we so palpably see how everything that befalls us continually turns out for the best. . . . Is there any more dangerous seduction than to renounce one's faith in [distant gods that don't concern themselves in human affairs] and to believe instead in some petty deity who is full of worries and personally knows every little hair on our heads and finds nothing nauseating in the most miserable small service?[26]

Having denied that God exists,[27] Nietzsche is saying, atheists must also deny that existence has any purpose.[28] Logically, they have to believe that life is ultimately chaotic and meaningless. There is no good and powerful deity directing the affairs of men; we are "free" to do what we want. The problem is that it *doesn't seem that way*. According to the plain appearance of things, someone *is* directing our lives for good. Therefore, in order to hold on to the belief that there is no god, we must deny what our senses tell us. Instead, Nietzsche goes on to write, we should either take credit ourselves for the good that befalls us or chalk it up to "beloved Chance: he leads our hand occasionally."[29]

Let's glance at a quick example to remind ourselves what this advice looks like in real life. Klaus Issler relates the story of Jason, a student of his who didn't have enough money to continue his doctoral studies. Jason prayed and asked God to provide the amount of his tuition bill: $2,117.60. A few days later his wife, Heather, was looking through some letters that her senile grandmother had written to her but never mailed. In them she found some bonds that totaled $2,000. That was amazing, but what was even more so was the fact that when they deposited the bonds in the bank, the actual figure turned out to be "$2,117.60! The bonds had appreciated."[30]

According to Nietzsche, Jason and Heather should either pat themselves on the back for so wisely providing for themselves, or be thankful that they just got lucky. And that is exactly the problem with naturalistic explanations of personal providence. Jason and Heather clearly did not provide the money for themselves, and if they just got lucky, *there is no one to thank*, even though the situation obviously and loudly cries out for gratitude. Skeptics may "thank their lucky stars" but does anyone think that is a rational sentiment?

That is why unbelievers so often anthropomorphize the concept of happenstance. Nietzsche used the pronoun *he* to talk about "beloved Chance"; others discuss supposedly random occurrences by thanking "Lady Luck" or "the hand of Fate." Why do they do this? Because the apparent reality of the situation is obviously personal and purposeful. It makes no sense to talk about blind chance as "leading our hand," but that sounds much less counterintuitive than to talk about our experiences of providence as if they were the result of impersonal, meaningless forces.

The natural reaction to Jason and Heather's story, as Nietzsche admitted, is to ascribe the act to a benevolent God. Naturalistic skeptics have to work hard to avoid this conclusion. Their worldview does a terrible job of accounting for the data of these experiences, so if they continue in their beliefs, it is *in spite of* the evidence, not because of it. That is the bottom line for many skeptics, a point we will focus on briefly in the next chapter.

Hypocrisy, Sex, and Other Causes of Skepticism

Frank Turek tells a story of what happened to his friend David. After David taught a class in apologetics, a young man approached him with an objection: "I once was a Christian, but now I'm an agnostic, and I don't think you should be doing what you're doing."

"What do you mean?" David asked.

"I don't think you should be giving arguments against atheists," the young man said. "Jesus told us to love, and what you're doing is not loving."

David started to answer the objection, but was met with several more in rapid-fire succession. (I spoke about this common tactic in chapter 2.) After trying in vain to answer a couple, David finally decided to end the charade and cut to the chase. He said, "You're raising all of these objections because you're sleeping with your girlfriend. Am I right?"

As Turek recounts, "All the blood drained from the kid's face. He was caught. He just stood there speechless. He was rejecting God because he didn't like God's morality, and he was disguising it with alleged intellectual objections."[1]

Now, please note that I am not recommending this as a typical example of how to properly end a conversation with a skeptic, as appropriate as it may have been in this particular case. I bring it up to point out that the arguments I have presented in this book are only going to get you so far. People are incredibly complex creatures, and doubt is usually rooted in a tangled ball of intellectual, psychological, emotional, and moral issues.

In this book we've stayed primarily in the intellectual realm. I've argued that unbelievers often need some help in the areas of theology, history, logic, and philosophy. We should, when necessary, gently instruct them in these subjects, using evidence and argument to help them see that the Christian worldview is more reasonable than all the alternatives. But even if you suc-ceed in convincing a person that your argument is sound and your worldview is true, that won't necessarily get him to become a Christian. There are myriad other factors at play, and we'll discuss a few of those in this chapter.

Before we get to that, though, I want to emphasize that just because rational discourse doesn't always get people to repent and turn to Jesus doesn't mean it's a waste of time. There are at least two major benefits to focusing on the more cerebral aspects of skepticism.

First, if the skeptic's doubts are primarily intellectual in na-ture, teaching her the truth should go a long way toward helping her change her mind. I don't know who started this saying, but I've heard it a lot: "No one's ever been argued into the king-dom." It's just not true. I recently read conversion stories by Edward Feser[2] and Kevin Vost.[3] Both were ardent atheists who became Christians after being overwhelmed by the weight of the philosophical arguments. As Feser explains,

> I don't know exactly when everything clicked. There was no single event, but a gradual transformation. As I taught and thought about the arguments for God's existence, and in particular the cosmological argument, I went from thinking "These arguments are no good" to thinking "These arguments are a little better than they are given credit for" and then to "These arguments are actually kind of interesting." Eventually it hit me: "Oh my goodness, these arguments are *right* after all!" By the summer of 2001 I would find myself trying to argue my wife's skeptical physicist brother-in-law into philosophical theism on the train the four of us were taking through Eastern Europe.[4]

C. S. Lewis had a similar conversion story.[5] Perhaps that is why Lewis was such an advocate of sound argumentation as an evangelistic tool. In *The Screwtape Letters*, the demon Screwtape warns his young apprentice not to try to use argument to keep people from God: "Jargon, not argument, is your best ally in keeping him from the Church. . . . The trouble with argument is that it moves the whole struggle onto the Enemy's own ground. . . . By the very act of arguing, you awake the patient's reason; and once it is awake, who can foresee the result?"[6]

We must not underestimate the power of the truth to jar a person out of a spiritual slumber. Sound theology and philosophy can have a wonderful effect on people. For example, Vost is sure that if he had known and understood the writings of Thomas Aquinas earlier in his life, he wouldn't have been an atheist so long.[7] That is an appraisal Feser, an Aquinas expert and advocate, would be sure to affirm.

Second, if the skeptic's doubts are not primarily intellectual, your conversation will make that clear. As you walk through the arguments, it should become obvious that the unbeliever is not rejecting God because religion is irrational or because "there just isn't enough evidence for Christianity." He may say that the problem is intellectual, but as you talk through the various positions, you will see that there are actually some other reasons keeping him from faith. Although that realization leaves much work still to be done, at least the facade will be down and you will better understand the nature of that task. You'll be able to focus on psychological, emotional, and moral factors that are actually driving the person's skepticism. To those issues we now turn.

Christians Behaving Badly

In *Why I Became an Atheist: A Former Preacher Rejects Christianity*, John Loftus explains that three major events in his life caused him to abandon his faith. He associates these events with three people: Linda, Larry, and Jeff. Linda was the co-worker with whom John had an affair, Larry was the professor of biochemistry who convinced John that the universe was billions of years old, and Jeff was one of the many pastors and church members with whom John had a series of conflicts. A vicious church split finally caused John to reach a breaking point: "The damage was done both psychologically in my experiences and intellectually as I continued to study the issues. Massive doubt crept upon me until I didn't want to be a part of any church much at all."[8]

Loftus's reasons for unbelief are quite typical. We've already addressed his intellectual and theological issues (the Larry factor) and we will talk about sex (the Linda factor) later in the chapter. For now, let's look at the Jeff factor: the issue of Christians acting immorally.

People who call themselves Christians can be jerks. There is just no way around this fact. Loftus tells about being really hurt by not getting a call from his pastor when he was down and out, but there are a million examples available. From sign-wielding preachers of hate yelling at gays, to motorists with fish stickers on their cars who cut people off and then flip them obscene hand gestures, believers don't always show much gentleness and compassion. After authoring *The End of Faith*, Sam Harris was motivated to write his *Letter to a Christian Nation* in part because he received so many letters telling him how wrong he was not to believe in God. He notes, "The most hostile of these communications have come from Christians. This is ironic, as Christians generally imagine that no faith imparts the virtues of love and forgiveness more effectively than their own. The truth is that many who claim to be transformed by Christ's love are deeply, even murderously, intolerant of criticism." [9]

How should we deal with skeptics who have been mistreated by Christians? Our first response should be to repent. There is no doubt that Christians are often immoral, and this does immense harm to the cause of Christ. As *Gaudium et Spes* (Pastoral Constitution on the Church [Joy and Hope]) points out, "Believers themselves often share some responsibility for [atheism]. . . . To the extent that they . . . fail in their religious, moral, or social life, they must be said to conceal rather than to reveal the true nature of God and of religion." [10] After reading John Loftus's book, Dr. Norman Geisler sent him a letter apologizing on "behalf of the body of Christ." Geisler noted that "the legalistic, unkind, and hypocritical way you were treated was simply unchristian and uncalled for. . . . There is no justification for unloving behavior on the part of Christians." [11] This is a good place to start.

You can also point out, though, that immorality by Christians is not actually a good reason to deny the truth of Christianity. For one thing, being a believer does not exempt one from having moral failures. As James Spiegel explains in detail in his book *Hypocrisy*,[12] being redeemed does not mean that Christians become perfect. Certainly God is moving us toward perfection, and we should be striving for that ideal, as we saw in chapter 6, but in this life we will always fall short of complete godliness. The fact that Christians still sin says nothing about whether Christianity is true.

Also, not everyone who acts in the name of God is a Christian. Jesus was very clear that we can know true Christians by their character:

> By their fruit you will recognize them. Do people pick grapes from thornbushes, or figs from thistles? Likewise, every good tree bears good fruit, but a bad tree bears bad fruit. A good tree cannot bear bad fruit, and a bad tree cannot bear good fruit. Every tree that does not bear good fruit is cut down and thrown into the fire. Thus, by their fruit you will recognize them.
>
> Matthew 7:16–20

He also said, "As I have loved you, so you must love one another. By this everyone will know that you are my disciples, if you love one another" (John 13:34–35). If a person claiming to be a Christian is completely unloving, there is cause to believe they are not truly a member of Christ's body.

Hypocrisy and general ungodliness play a major part in skepticism. If your conversation partner seems more resistant to Christians than Jesus or Christianity, it may be because she has been hurt by believers in the past.

Heartbreak

When Russell Baker was five years old, his father was suddenly taken to the hospital and died. As the *New York Times* columnist recounts in his best-selling autobiography, it was a pivotal event in his life:

> For the first time I thought seriously about God. Between sobs I told [the family housekeeper] Bessie that if God could do things like this to people, then God was hateful and I had no more use for Him.
>
> Bessie told me about the peace of Heaven and the joy of being among the angels and the happiness of my father who was already there. This argument failed to quiet my rage.
>
> "God loves us all just like His own children," Bessie said.
>
> "If God loves me, why did He make my father die?"
>
> Bessie said that I would understand someday, but she was only partly right. That afternoon, though I couldn't have phrased it this way then, I decided that God was a lot less interested in people than anybody in Morrisonville was willing to admit. That day I decided that God was not entirely to be trusted.
>
> After that I never cried again with any real conviction, nor expected much of anyone's God except indifference, nor loved deeply without fear that it would cost me dearly in pain. At the age of five I had become a skeptic.[13]

Baker's heartbreaking (and all too common) story is quite revealing in regard to the psychology of skepticism. I'm sure most of us can think of someone we know who is angry at God about some tragedy in his life. Often, it seems, this goes hand in hand with a denial of God's very existence. A recent study led by psychologist Julie Exline of Case Western Reserve University supports this notion. In studying college students, her research indicated that "atheists and agnostics reported more anger at God during their lifetimes than believers. A separate study also found this pattern among bereaved individuals."[14] If atheists and agnostics are angry at *God*, what does that say about their skepticism? It seems to suggest that the intellectual label they wear is motivated by their hurt more than rational analysis of the evidence.

Fatherlessness

Baker's situation, unfortunately, made him particularly prone to such a reaction. As Paul Vitz argues in his provocative and persuasive book *Faith of the Fatherless*,[15] the absence of a father, or presence of a defective father (e.g., one who is abusive or weak or cowardly) can play a major role in young men becoming atheists.

Vitz's "defective father hypothesis" suggests that a broken relationship with one's father makes it very difficult to accept a supposedly loving father in heaven. Vitz developed this theory while studying the lives of history's "great" atheists, including Hume, Schopenhauer, Nietzsche, Russell, Sartre, Camus, Hobbes, Voltaire, Butler, and Freud. All either had fathers who died when they were very young or were "defective" in some major way. James Spiegel notes that this principle also applies to many modern-day skeptics as well, including Daniel Dennett and Christopher Hitchens.[16]

Of course, this does not mean that all fatherless kids will become atheists, and there are many qualifications and subtleties to Vitz's argument that I won't get into here. However, his point is something to keep in mind when talking to skeptics. Humans naturally conceive of God according to the pattern set for us by human fathers. When that father isn't there or isn't loving, "an atheist's disappointment in and resentment of his own father unconsciously justifies his rejection of God."[17] In a culture where a third of our children are growing up without their biological dad and 40 percent of babies are born to unwed mothers,[18] you can expect to run into this problem more often in the future.

Social Pressures

Vitz himself became an atheist in college and offers a frank assessment of his motives: "On reflection, I have seen that my reasons for becoming, and remaining, an atheist-skeptic from age eighteen to age thirty-eight were, on the whole, superficial and lacking in serious intellectual and moral foundation."[19] He notes that he accepted the ideas presented to him by academics without ever actually studying them or questioning them in any way. So why did he accept them? One reason was "social unease."[20] Vitz was embarrassed to be from the Midwest, which "seemed terribly dull, narrow, and provincial" compared to the big city. He wanted to "take part, to be comfortable, in the new, glamorous secular world" into which he was moving, as did many of his classmates.[21] He also wanted to be accepted within his scientific field, so just as he had learned to dress like a college student by putting on the right clothes, he learned to "think like a proper psychologist by putting on the right—that is, atheistic—ideas and attitudes."[22]

Michael Shermer, editor-in-chief of *Skeptics Magazine* and executive director of The Skeptics Society, has a similar explanation for his de-conversion story:

> Socially, when I moved from theism to atheism, and science as a worldview, I guess, to be honest, I just liked the people in science, and the scientists, and their books, and just the lifestyle, and the way of living. I liked that better than the religious books, the religious people I was hanging out with—just socially. It just felt more comfortable for me. . . . In reality, I think most of us arrive at most of our beliefs for non-rational reasons, and then we justify them with these reasons after the fact.[23]

Well, I'm not sure if most people do that or not, but it is clearly a bad way to arrive at answers about the big questions of life.

Skeptics who practice this method are not evaluating evidence and making reasoned decisions. They are choosing a worldview because they like how it makes them feel to be accepted into the "in" group.

The Cost of Discipleship

G. K. Chesterton famously said, "The Christian ideal has not been tried and found wanting. It has been found difficult; and left untried."[24] That sums up another reason for skepticism: Following Jesus is hard!

For example, Vitz admits that "personal inconvenience" was another major factor in his atheism: "Religion takes a good deal of time, not just on Sunday mornings; the serious practice of any religion calls for much more than that. There are other church services, as well as time for prayer and Scripture reading, not to mention time for 'good works' of various sorts. I was far too busy for such time-consuming activities."[25]

Philosopher Mortimer Adler became a Christian while in his eighties, after spending decades refusing to make that commitment. During that time he admitted that converting to a specific faith would simply be too hard for him. It "would require a radical change in the way of my life, a basic alteration in the direction of my day-to-day choices as well as in the ultimate objectives to be sought or hoped for. . . . The simple truth of the matter is that I did not wish to live up to being a genuinely religious person."[26]

In cases like this, skepticism is simply the rationalization of a desire to stay comfortable. People don't want to take on the commitment that becoming a Christian requires, so they claim that it must be false.

Pope John Paul II noted that this attitude can also lead to resentment and even hatred of religion.

The fact is that attaining or realizing a higher value demands a greater effort of will. So in order to spare ourselves the effort, to excuse our failure to obtain this value, we minimize its significance, deny it the respect that it deserves, even see it as in some way evil.[27]

That would certainly help explain some of the contempt we see for Christianity among modern skeptics. If you run into an unbeliever who offers scorn rather than reasoned arguments, this may be why.

Immorality

Now, for the big one. Of all the motivations and reasons for skepticism that I encounter, immorality is easily the most common. In particular, sexual sin seems to be the largest single factor driving disbelief in our culture. Brant Hansen calls sex "The Big But" because he so often hears this from unbelievers: "'I like Jesus, BUT . . .' and the 'but' is usually followed, one way or the other, with an objection about the Bible and . . . sex. People think something's deeply messed-up with a belief system that says two consenting, unmarried adults should refrain from sex."[28] In other words, people simply do not want to follow the Christian teaching that sexual intercourse should take place only between a man and woman who are married, so they throw the whole religion out.

Why is sex such a big deal for skeptics? You might think it is a bit like the social pressure factor. Sex feels even better than being welcomed into a group, so we choose to live promiscuous lives rather than admit that there might be a God who doesn't want us to do so. However, I believe there is much more to it than that. Sex is in a special category all its own.

To make that case, let's start by discussing how immorality in general relates to skepticism.

As I wrote in part 2, to sin is to rebel against the nature of reality.[29] Sinning is not about breaking some arbitrary and capricious rule; it is to live contrary to the inherent order and purpose of the world. For example, I talked about the man who worshiped and served alcohol rather than his wife and kids. This is immoral. However, it is not wrong because he broke some arbitrary statute God made up against excessive drinking or because he didn't live according to the random advice found in some parenting guru's *Handbook for Dads*. It is wrong because this action is contrary to the inherent nature of fathers, husbands, wives, children, and alcohol. The man's wife and kids are objectively and innately more valuable than booze, and the inherent purpose of a husband and a father is to give of himself for their good by protecting and providing for them, among other duties.

To reject the natural order of things is sin. It is a denial of reality. As Chesterton wrote, the only sin is to call a green leaf gray.[30] It is to say to the creator of the world, "I will not accept the world as you made it. I don't want to submit to reality. I want to make my own reality. I want to determine my own meaning in life and live by my own value system. I refuse to accept my status as creature. I want to be the creator. I want to be God."

This is an important starting point for our discussion of sin and skepticism, because the easiest way to justify sin, then, is to deny that there is a creator to provide reality with nature, thereby denying that there is any inherent order and purpose in the universe.

Let's say I'm the dad who would prefer to drink away my paycheck rather than take care of my family, and I am looking for a way to defend that choice. One simple method would be to argue that "fatherhood" has no inherent meaning; it's just an arbitrary cultural construction. Thus, I can live however I want. Indeed, I may go further and posit that the traditional notion of fatherhood is constraining me from living life to the fullest. The whole idea was probably developed by evil church authorities as a way to consolidate power. I need to throw off the shackles of this capricious and harmful restriction and find true "freedom" apart from my family (as they do not have any more objective value than anything else anyway). So I deny that God exists. This leaves the universe purposeless and enables me to do whatever I want. Voilà! Suddenly I'm a skeptic.

Aldous Huxley admitted that this is a common reason for skepticism:

> I had motives for not wanting the world to have a meaning; consequently I assumed that it had none and was able without any difficulty to find satisfying reasons for this assumption. . . . Those who detect no meaning in the world generally do so because, for one reason or another, it suits their books that the world should be meaningless. . . .
>
> For myself as, no doubt, for most of my contemporaries, the philosophy of meaninglessness was essentially an instrument of liberation. The liberation we desired was simultaneously liberation from a certain political and economic system and liberation from a certain system of morality. We objected to the morality because it interfered with our sexual freedom; we objected to the political system because it was unjust. The supporters of these systems claimed that in some way they embodied the meaning (a Christian meaning, they insisted) of the world. There was one admirably simple method in our political and erotic revolt: We could deny that the world had any meaning whatsoever. Similar tactics had been adopted during the eighteenth century and for the same reasons.[31]

Indeed, similar tactics have been used extensively up to the present day. If you are looking for two great resources that document the extent to which the work of the world's "great" atheistic thinkers has been "calculated to justify or minimize the shame of their own debauchery,"[32] I recommend *Intellectuals* by Paul Johnson[33] and *Degenerate Moderns: Modernity as Rationalized Sexual Misbehavior* by E. Michael Jones.[34] Also, James Spiegel has a nice summary of their arguments in *The Making of an Atheist.*[35] The bottom line is that these skeptical scholars didn't reach their conclusions by following the evidence where it led. They didn't "discover" that the world was meaningless and then proceed to live accordingly. They lived sinful lives (usually involving some type of sexual deviancy) and then produced theories that justified their actions.

This connection between immorality and unsound thought is clearly scriptural. Paul tells the Ephesians that they

> must no longer live as the Gentiles do, in the futility of their thinking. They are darkened in their understanding and separated from the life of God because of the ignorance that is in them due to the hardening of their hearts. Having lost all sensitivity, they have given themselves over to sensuality so as to indulge in every kind of impurity, with a continual lust for more.
>
> Ephesians 4:17–19 NIV1984

Paul blames futile thinking and a lack of understanding on hard hearts. When we compare this passage with Romans 1, it seems that immorality and bad ideas work together in a vicious cycle that spirals downward. Sin leads to false philosophies, which then lead to more sin.

> The wrath of God is being revealed from heaven against all the godlessness and wickedness of men who suppress the truth by their wickedness, since what may be known about God is plain to them, because God has made it plain to them. For since the creation of the world God's invisible qualities—his eternal power

and divine nature—have been clearly seen, being understood from what has been made, so that men are without excuse.

For although they knew God, they neither glorified him as God nor gave thanks to him, but their thinking became futile and their foolish hearts were darkened. Although they claimed to be wise, they became fools and exchanged the glory of the immortal God for images made to look like mortal man and birds and animals and reptiles.

Therefore God gave them over in the sinful desires of their hearts to sexual impurity for the degrading of their bodies with one another. They exchanged the truth of God for a lie, and worshiped and served created things rather than the Creator— who is forever praised.

Romans 1:18–25 NIV1984

So Paul argues that the nature of reality is clear to everyone but people *"suppress the truth by their wickedness."* Rebellious people become fools as they deny the obvious meaning of creation because of their sin. Their foolishness leads them to indulge in more immorality. For example, according to Romans 1, everyone knows, at a deep, foundational level, that women and children are more important than alcohol. This is a clear, objective fact about reality. However, the sinful man denies this truth, and in the process becomes a fool, in order to assuage his guilt and indulge in disordered desires. Thus immorality is very closely linked to skepticism, and we need to be aware that sin will almost always be at least an underlying issue in our conversations.

Why Sex Is Such a Big Deal

If immorality is a cause of skepticism, are there any specific sins that cause more problems than others? Yes. Sexual immorality is perhaps the premier cause of skepticism. You don't generally see people denying Christianity because they want to justify their gluttony or anger issues but, as we've already seen in several examples, they often reject God based on their sexual proclivities. Indeed, my fictional example about denying God based on alcohol may ring a bit false to you for this very reason. People don't usually become atheists because they have a drinking problem. However, if the same story had the man spending all his time and money on a mistress rather than alcohol, it becomes much more plausible, doesn't it?

The question is *why*. Here's the answer: Sexual immorality is more often related to skepticism than, say, greed or gossip or alcoholism because it constitutes a more radical and serious rebellion against the natural order. This brings a greater degree of dissonance and guilt and a stronger motivation for denying that a natural order exists.

To flesh that out a bit, the true meaning of sex is very obvious,[36] and it is very good. As we will discuss momentarily, sex provides us with knowledge of the meaning of life and an experiential insight into the very nature of God. However, because sex provides such an important and powerful revelation, to reject that truth is to rebel against the natural order on a scale far greater than most other sins. To take part in adultery, homosexuality, or abortion,[37] for example, is a greater rejection of God than being a gossip because these actions involve openly rebelling against truth that is so obvious and so holy. As we look at the meaning of sex, we will see more clearly why trying to live contrary to its true nature is such a serious offense.

Sex Reveals the Meaning of Life

We saw in chapter 4 that the meaning of life is love. We were created to give of ourselves to others for their good. Have you ever wondered how Adam and Eve knew this? After all, they didn't have any books to read or Internet sites to surf. I suppose they could have just asked God directly, but somehow I don't think that was necessary. Adam and Eve knew that life was all about love because they could see each other naked (Genesis 2:25). They knew from the very form and nature of their bodies that they were made to give of themselves to each other. One doesn't have to be a great detective to see how male and female bodies were designed to go together and that this involves an act of mutual self-giving.

John Paul II calls this the "nuptial meaning of the body." He explains "The body includes right from the beginning . . . the capacity of expressing love, that love in which the person becomes a gift—and by means of this gift—fulfills the meaning of his being and existence."[38] Adam and Eve could see that they were meant to have sex, and that this truth was inseparable from the fact that they were meant to love. As Matthew Lee Anderson writes:

> In the act of sex itself, the man gives himself to the woman and the woman (by way of freely opening herself) gives herself to the man. In that sense, Christian sexuality is not simply an expression of an abstract or vague inner desire—it is a dynamic encounter between a man and a woman in the fullness of their humanity before God, which is constituted by their mutual self-giving to the other for the other's good.[39]

As Dietrich von Hildebrand notes, "The sexual gift of one person to another signifies an incomparably close union with that other and a self-surrender to him or her. The sexual union is thus the organic expression of wedded love, which intends precisely this mutual gift of self."[40] In nuptial sex man and woman give themselves to each other completely and totally;

nothing is withheld. Their bodies and spirits are given to each other in full self-surrender. This is true love. Anderson continues,

> Authentic human sexuality is something more than a physical act done for the purpose of bodily stimulation or pleasure. It is the mutual self-giving of two persons in their external dimensions, inaugurating a union that encompasses the totality of their lives. It is an overflow of love that starts in the heart and shows itself in the very members of our flesh.[41]

Sex Reveals the Nature of Life in the Trinity

We also saw in chapter 4 that the meaning of life is not arbitrary. It's not as if God had several different options to choose from and finally decided on "love" as the purpose he would impose on humans. Love is the meaning of life because God is love. We are called to interpersonal communion because God himself is a communion of persons in the Trinity.[42]

Indeed, to be in communion with another person is one part of what it means to be created in the image of God. Genesis 1:27 states: "So God created mankind in his own image, in the image of God he created them; male and female he created them." That is why Adam was incomplete without Eve. He could not reflect the image of God without Eve to love. The image of God is not found in Adam alone or in Eve alone, but in the union of Adam and Eve.

The sexual union of Adam and Eve is the clearest image we have of the life of the Trinity. Nuptial sex, then, is about as close as we are going to get on earth to experiencing the complete mutual self-giving that takes place within the persons of the godhead. But someday we will experience that Trinitarian life fully. Sex, therefore, is a foretaste of heaven. I have said throughout this book that the culmination of God's redemptive purposes is to draw us into the life of the Trinity. God intends for us to partake of his very essence for eternity. The clearest physical picture we get of that blissful state is sex. Of course physical sex on earth will pale in comparison to the spiritual intimacy we will share with God in heaven. The great mystics who have tasted of both testify to this. However, physical intimacy does offer us a small clue. Peter Kreeft writes:

> This spiritual intercourse with God is the ecstasy hinted at in all earthly intercourse, physical or spiritual. It is the ultimate reason why sexual passion is so strong, so different from other passions, so heavy with suggestions of profound meanings that just elude our grasp. No mere practical needs account for it. No mere animal drive explains it. No animal falls in love, writes profound romantic poetry, or sees sex as a symbol of the ultimate meaning of life because no animal is made in the image of God. *Human* sexuality is that image, and human sexuality is a foretaste of that self-giving, that losing and finding the self, that oneness-in-manyness that is the heart of the life and joy of the Trinity. That is what we long for; that is why we tremble to stand outside ourselves in the other, to give our whole selves, body and soul: because we are images of God the sexual being. We love the other sex because God loves God.[43]

Sex Enables Us to Participate in God's Creative Activity

Love is inherently creative; it cannot be contained. The joining of two persons in love results in more people to love. I believe this admittedly mysterious principle of reality was at work in the creation of the world and continues to be at work in the creative process that sustains the world. God did not start everything and then leave it to operate by its own power. He continually upholds it by his power. If God stopped his creative work, all life would cease. Amazingly, humans get to play a part in this process. Being made in the image of God includes the ability to participate with him in creating new life. It makes sense, of course, that this life would come as a result of sex. Just as Adam and Eve were created out of God's love, their children are created out of their love.

Why Sexual Immorality Is So Bad

If the meaning of sex is to practice love and share in the life of God, then the reason for the biblical injunction that sex should only be practiced between a man and a woman who are married becomes far more clear: That is the only place the fulfillment of sex's purpose could take place.

For example, sex is about love. But extramarital sexual affairs are not about love. They are about each person using the other as a means of physical pleasure. This is not love. Love by its nature is the giving of self for the other's good. Sex outside of marriage is about making another person a tool for self-gratification. Even if the sex partners genuinely care about each other (and frankly, usually illicit sex is very explicitly about selfish desires: "I have a right to be happy"; "He just makes me feel so good about myself"; "We just hooked up for the night because it was fun," and so on), sex without marriage is not a complete self-gift. Something of each person is always withheld, not the least of which is lifelong commitment.

Also, sex outside of marriage removes the image of God from the equation and keeps us from participating in the Trinity. The fullness of God's nature and creative plan is experienced in the sacrament of marriage only. It is impossible in homosexual or adulterous relationships. These practices, as well as other sexual sins, disavow God by their very essence. They are a blatant and aggressive slap in his face, so to speak.

As such, they have a great effect on other areas of life. After all, if a person is willing to deny the obvious meaning of sex, to what part of the natural order will they conform? In other words, if they won't affirm and submit to the natural order in this area, they have essentially rejected the natural order in all areas, thereby making any and every action morally acceptable. Feser notes that abortion and homosexuality have traditionally been regarded with such horror not because they are worse than other sins on some scale of judgment but because they are positively unnatural and

> they constitute an affront to the foundations of morality. If there is no such thing as a natural order . . . then there can be no basis for morality at all. But those who commit an act of sodomy or abortion seem to thumb their nose at the very idea of natural order, to put themselves above and beyond it.[44]

I believe this is one reason why, in the passage above from Romans, Paul lists "sexual immorality" as the first consequence of foolishness and idolatry. He follows that with a longer list of vices, but gives preeminence to homosexuality before moving on to iniquities such as envy and even murder.

> Because of this, God gave them over to shameful lusts. Even their women exchanged natural sexual relations for unnatural ones. In the same way the men also abandoned natural relations with women and were inflamed with lust for one another. Men committed shameful acts with other men, and received in themselves the due penalty for their error.
>
> Furthermore, just as they did not think it worthwhile to retain the knowledge of God, so God gave them over to a depraved mind, so that they do what ought not to be done. They have

become filled with every kind of wickedness, evil, greed and depravity. They are full of envy, murder, strife, deceit and malice. They are gossips, slanderers, God-haters, insolent, arrogant and boastful; they invent ways of doing evil; they disobey their parents; they have no understanding, no fidelity, no love, no mercy. Although they know God's righteous decree that those who do such things deserve death, they not only continue to do these very things but also approve of those who practice them.

Romans 1:26–32

Sex is intended to be the source of great light in our world. Sexual immorality, however, leads down an increasingly dark path. It seems that once a person has embarked on that road, there is a point at which the easiest way to justify himself is to simply deny that God exists. That is one reason sexual immorality is perhaps the major cause of skepticism.

Telling the World Its Story

I opened this book by saying that religious skepticism is on the rise. However, as we have seen, this is not primarily due to the intellectual power or persuasive energy of any anti-Christian worldview. Today's most vocal unbelievers are not rejecting Christianity based on a reasoned attempt to explain the evidence in some other way. Their attacks on the faith are not well-thought-out and substantial arguments, but propaganda assaults that don't stand much scrutiny, and cannot compete in an honest marketplace of ideas.[1] This should give us confidence as we interact with our skeptical friends and colleagues. You may not have all the answers, but they certainly don't either. By asking questions and gently instructing them in the truth, you can be used by God to open their minds and hearts to his love.

You can also be encouraged by the fact that you have the answers that unbelievers need, whether they realize it or not. As Richard John Neuhaus notes, "Our job is to alert people to their own story."[2] God has entrusted us with the task of telling the world the truth about the meaning of life, the source of evil, and the wonderful plan God has enacted to fix it. That truth is exactly what people need to make sense of their lives, and whether they acknowledge that over coffee with you or not, it is still a fact. Telling that story will have an effect.

Indeed, right now Christians have a unique opportunity to multiply that effect as Christianity currently has no strong worldview competitors. Neuhaus writes, "At this beginning of the third millennium, there is only one comprehensive, coherent, compelling, hopeful story of the human project being proposed to the world, and that is the Gospel of Jesus Christ."[3]

People are searching for their story. They long to make sense of this world and find some reason for hope. We have the truth they are looking for. God has given us an amazing opportunity and we must take advantage of it. My prayer is that you are now better equipped to do just that.

Notes

Introduction: How to Reach a Culture of Radical Unbelief

1. "Science, 'Frauds' Trigger a Decline in Atheism," *The Washington Times*, March 3, 2005, www.washingtontimes.com/news/2005/mar/3/20050303-115733 -9519r/.

2. The editors suggested that atheism was in decline because it was losing its scientific underpinnings and atheists themselves were no more moral than religious people. On one hand, advances in physics and biology provide evidence of a designer rather than random processes as their source, and on the other, atheism has, to quote Alistar McGrath in the same article, "turned out to have just as many frauds, psychopaths and careerists as religion does."

3. Kimberly Winston, "Poll Shows Atheism on the Rise in the US," *The Washington Post*, August 13, 2012, http://articles.washingtonpost.com/2012-08-13 /national/35491519_1_new-atheism-atheist-groups-new-atheists.

4. Kimberly Winston, "9/11 Gave Birth to Aggressive, Unapologetic 'New Atheists,'" *The Christian Century*, August 27, 2011, www.christiancentury.org /article/2011-08/911-gave-birth-aggressive-unapologetic-new-atheists.

Chapter 1: No Selling Required

1. "U.S. Religious Landscape Survey Summary of Key Findings," *The Pew Forum on Religion and Public Life*, http://religions.pewforum.org/reports.

2. Timothy Shriver, "Shopping for God," *The Washington Post*, March 10, 2008, http://newsweek.washingtonpost.com/onfaith/religionfromtheheart/2008/03 /shopping_for_god.html.

3. Ibid.

4. Stacy Weiner, "A Leap of Faith," *The Washington Post*, May 9, 2006, www.washingtonpost.com/wp-dyn/content/article/2006/05/08/AR2006050801012.html.

5. Cathy Lynn Grossman, "Make-Your-Own Religion? More and More Americans Are Doing It, According to New Book 'Futurecast,'" *Huffington Post*, September 15, 2011, www.huffingtonpost.com/2011/09/15/make-your-own-religion_n_964570.html.

6. "Bishop Orders Episcopal Priest to Renounce Islamic Faith," *USA Today*, March 15, 2009, http://usatoday30.usatoday.com/news/religion/2009-03-15-priest_N.htm.

7. Weiner, "A Leap of Faith."

8. Sam Harris, *Letter to a Christian Nation* (New York: Vintage, 2006), 46–47.

9. C. S. Lewis, *God in the Dock* (London: Fount Paperbacks, 1979), 67.

10. Dorothy Sayers, *Creed or Chaos: Why Christians Must Choose Either Dogma or Disaster* (Manchester, NH: Sophia Institute Press, 1995), 44.

Chapter 2: The Big Picture

1. The Don Johnson Radio Show, March 13, 2005, audio available at donjohnsonministries.org.

2. Daniel C. Dennett, "The Bright Stuff," *New York Times*, July 12, 2003, www.nytimes.com/2003/07/12/opinion/the-bright-stuff.html.

3. Richard Dawkins, *The Selfish Gene*, 2nd ed. (Oxford: Oxford University Press, 1989), 198.

4. Richard Dawkins, *The God Delusion* (Boston: Houghton Mifflin, 2006), 347.

5. Thomas Dubay, *Faith and Certitude* (San Francisco: Ignatius, 1985), 111–112.

6. Gregory Koukl, *Tactics: A Game Plan for Discussing Your Christian Convictions* (Grand Rapids, MI: Zondervan, 2009), 62.

7. For example, Tom Clark of the Center for Naturalism (www.centerfornaturalism.org) is an atheist who argues that most atheists spend too much time simply attacking Christianity rather than presenting a comprehensive worldview alternative. You can hear him present this case on the January 22, 2009 episode of the *Reasonable Doubts* podcast: http://feedproxy.google.com/~r/reasonabledoubts/Msxh/~5/6LlLky6z23M/rd30_fwvd2_judgement_day_with_guest_tom_clark.mp3.

Chapter 3: The State of the Doubter's Knowledge

1. Hugh Hewitt, *In, But Not Of: A Guide to Christian Ambition* (Nashville: Thomas Nelson, 2003), 172–173.

2. Koukl, *Tactics,* 48.

3. Randy Newman, *Questioning Evangelism: Engaging People's Hearts the Way Jesus Did* (Grand Rapids, MI: Kregel, 2004), 42.

4. Lewis, *God in the Dock,* 97.

5. Douglas Groothuis, *Christian Apologetics: A Comprehensive Case for Biblical Faith* (Downers Grove, IL: InterVarsity Press Academic, 2011), 116.

Chapter 4: Love and the Meaning of Life

1. Edward Current, "An Atheist Meets God," YouTube, www.youtube.com /watch?v=urlTBBKTO68.

2. Thomas Jefferson, quoted in Richard Dawkins, *The God Delusion* (New York: Mariner Books, 2008), 51.

3. Richard Dawkins, *The God Delusion* (New York: Mariner Books, 2008), 51.

4. For example, see Alistar McGrath's *The Dawkins Delusion* (Downers Grove, IL: InterVarsity Press Books, 2007). Along with his own critique of Dawkins, McGrath cites many others who are "embarrassed" by Dawkins' theology.

5. Terry Eagleton, "Lunging, Flailing, Mispunching: A Review of Richard Dawkins' *The God Delusion*," *London Review of Books*, October 19, 2006.

6. Rodney Stark, *What Americans Really Believe* (Waco, TX: Baylor University Press, 2008), 120.

7. Edward Feser, *The Last Superstition* (South Bend, IN: St. Augustine's Press, 2008), 4.

8. Dawkins, *The God Delusion*, 15.

9. Jean Daniélou, *God and the Ways of Knowing* (San Francisco: Ignatius Press, 2003), 122.

Chapter 5: The Reason for the Rules

1. Rick Reilly, "The Grinch Who Stole the Homer" *ESPN The Magazine*, June 29, 2009, http://sports.espn.go.com/espn/columns/story?columnist =reilly_rick&id=4263659.

2. Gordon Graham, "Kindergartner Suspended for Bringing Toy Gun to School," Fox19, Nov. 9, 2011, www.fox19.com/story/16003464/kindergartner-suspended -for-bringing-toy-gun-to-school.

3. Christopher Hitchens, *God Is Not Great* (New York: Twelve, 2007), 212.

4. Ibid.

5. Ibid., 111–112.

Chapter 6: What Jesus Meant by That Whole "Born Again" Thing

1. For a fuller discussion of the poll data, see Ronald J. Sider, *The Scandal of the Evangelical Conscience* (Grand Rapids, MI: Baker, 2005).

2. Sider, *The Scandal of the Evangelical Conscience*, 17.

3. Jean Daniélou, *The Bible and the Liturgy* (Notre Dame, IN: University of Notre Dame Press, 1956), 75.

4. See also Psalm 74:13 and Psalm 77:16.

5. Optatus of Milan, *Donat*, V, 1; PL, 11, 1041, quoted in Jean Daniélou, "The Sacraments and the History of Salvation," www.catholicculture.org/culture/library /view.cfm?recnum=681.

6. Esther was a type of Jesus in that she also was a member of two families who interceded with the king to save her people. Esther was a Jewish girl who won a contest and became King Xerxes' queen (Esther 1–2). Xerxes did not know at the time that Esther was Jewish, so when Haman, a trusted nobleman close to the king, devised a plot to kill all the Jews in the land, Xerxes went along with it (Esther

3:6–15). Esther's cousin Mordecai convinced her that she had to do something to stop the annihilation of her people, and Esther bravely went before the king to intercede on their behalf (Esther 4:1–5:2). There are many more interesting twists and turns within the biblical account, but the bottom line is that Esther's plea was successful and the Jews were saved (Esther 5:3–9:17). Just as he had done with Moses, God providentially placed Esther in the royal family so she could have access to the seat of power when that became necessary to save the Israelites. Both Moses and Esther are people who illuminate Jesus, the one who has membership in the divine royal family necessary to save us.

7. Richard White, "Justification As Divine Sonship," in Scott Hahn, *Catholic for a Reason: Scripture and the Mystery of the Family of God*, Leon Suprenant, ed. (Steubenville, OH: Emmaus Road Publishing, 1998), 107.

8. Scott Hahn, "The Mystery of the Family of God," in Hahn, *Catholic for a Reason*, 11.

Chapter 7: Why Hell Is Fair and Heaven Won't Be Boring

1. James Lileks, *Notes of a Nervous Man* (New York: Pocket Books, 1991), 167.

2. Dallas Willard, *Renovation of the Heart: Putting On the Character of Christ* (Colorado Springs: NavPress, 2002), 59.

3. Regis Martin, *The Last Things* (San Francisco: Ignatius Press, 1998), 92.

4. C. S. Lewis, *The Great Divorce* (New York: HarperCollins, 2009), 75.

5. Peter Kreeft, *Fundamentals of the Faith: Essays in Christian Apologetics* (San Francisco: Ignatius, 1988), 163, excerpt available at www.peterkreeft.com /topics/hell.htm.

6. Peter Kreeft and Ronald K. Tacelli, *Handbook of Christian Apologetics* (Downers Grove, IL: InterVarsity Press, 1994), 289.

7. Joseph Ratzinger, *Eschatology—Death and Eternal Life*, trans. by Michael Waldstein (Washington, DC: Catholic University of America Press, 1988), 206.

8. Kreeft and Tacelli, *Handbook of Christian Apologetics,* 290.

9. Ibid.

10. Dr. Reaps, "Emmanuel Kelly, The X Factor 2011 Auditions, Emmanuel Kelly FULL," www.youtube.com/watch?v=W86jlvrG54o.

11. David Kerr, "*X Factor* star gives credit for success to Catholic mom," Catholic News Agency, Oct. 25, 2011, www.catholicnewsagency.com/news /x-factor-star-gives-credit-for-success-to-his-catholic-mom/.

12. C. S. Lewis, *Mere Christianity* (San Francisco: HarperCollins, 2001), 134.

13. William Shakespeare, *Macbeth*, Act V, Scene V.

14. G. K. Beale, *A New Testament Biblical Theology: The Unfolding of the Old Testament in the New* (Grand Rapids, MI: Baker Academic, 2011), 58.

15. Kreeft, *Fundamentals*, 160–161.

16. Joel Stein, "A little bit of heaven on earth," *Los Angeles Times,* Dec. 21, 2007, www.latimes.com/news/la-oe-stein21dec21,0,6843058.column.

17. Peter Kreeft, *The God Who Loves You: "Love Divine, All Loves Excelling"* (San Francisco: Ignatius Press, 2004), 88.

18. Randy Alcorn, *Heaven* (Wheaton, IL: Tyndale, 2004), inside cover.

19. Martin, *The Last Things,* 109.

Chapter 8: How to Think About the Bible

1. Dan Brown, *The Da Vinci Code* (New York: Anchor Books, 2006), 250.

2. Russell Pregeant, *Reading the Bible for All the Wrong Reasons* (Minneapolis, MN: Augsburg Fortress Press, 2011), 2, excerpted at *Ministry Matters,* www.ministry matters.com/all/article/entry/1611/reading-the-bible-for-all-the-wrong-reasons.

3. Jim Merritt, "A List of Biblical Contradictions," infidels.org, www.infidels .org/library/modern/jim_merritt/bible-contradictions.html.

4. Ibid.

5. Dan Barker, *Losing Faith in Faith: From Preacher to Atheist* (Madison, WI: Freedom from Religion Foundation, 1992), 164, excerpted at http://ffrf.org/legacy/ books/lfif/?t=contra.

6. Ibid.

7. Roger Olson, *The Mosaic of Christian Belief* (Downers Grove, IL: Inter-Varsity Press, 2002), 75.

8. Vishal Mangalwadi, "Why Christianity Lost America," Revelation Movement, December 10, 2011, www.revelationmovement.com/instructors/blog_post/38.

9. Ibid.

10. *Dogmatic Constitution on Divine Revelation* (Boston: Pauline Books and Media, 1965), 4.

11. Ibid.

12. Olson, *The Mosaic of Christian Belief,* 73.

13. C. S. Lewis, *Letters of C. S. Lewis* (Boston: Houghton Mifflin Harcourt, 2003), 247.

14. *Dogmatic Constitution on Divine Revelation,* 16.

15. Michael J. Christensen, *C. S. Lewis on Scripture: His Thoughts on the Nature of Biblical Inspiration, The Role of Revelation and the Question of Inerrancy* (Waco, Texas: Word, 1979), 96.

16. John Webster, *Holy Scripture: A Dogmatic Sketch* (Cambridge, England: Cambridge University Press, 2003), 36, italics added for emphasis.

17. The Pontifical Biblical Commission, *The Interpretation of the Bible in the Church* (Boston: Pauline Books and Media, 1993), 133.

18. Harris, *Letter to a Christian Nation,* 60.

19. Ibid., 61.

20. Kreeft and Tacelli, *Handbook of Christian Apologetics,* 207.

21. This is not to say that we need to accept all the methods and philosophical presuppositions of the historical critical method used by such groups as the Jesus Seminar. The problem with their approach is not so much the idea of wanting to get to the "historical Jesus," but that they work within an unsupported naturalistic framework.

22. "Frequently Asked Questions," *Losing My Religion,* http://losingmyreligion .com/faq.htm.

23. Ibid.

24. Ibid.

25. For a good discussion of the necessity of interpretation, see chapter 1 of *How to Read the Bible for All Its Worth* by Gordon D. Fee and Douglas Stuart (Grand Rapids, MI: Zondervan, 1993).

26. Olson, *The Mosaic of Christian Belief,* 67.

27. Pregeant, excerpted at www.ministrymatters.com/all/article/entry/1611 /reading-the-bible-for-all-the-wrong-reasons.

28. The anagogical refers to the fulfillment of God's plan, but that fulfillment can already be present in some form. The New Jerusalem is already here in a certain sense in our worship, for example, but it is not present in its fullness.

29. Joe Kovacs, "Did Jesus actually reveal name of the Antichrist?" *WorldNet-Daily*, July 30, 2009, www.wnd.com/index.php?pageId=105527.

30. Ibid.

Chapter 9: The God Hypothesis

1. The Don Johnson Show, "Discussion with Jason the Ex-Christian," August 1, 2011, available at http://donjohnsonministries.org/discussion-with -jason-the-ex-christian/.

2. Groothuis, *Christian Apologetics,* 45.

3. Mitch Stokes, *A Shot of Faith (to the Head): Be a Confident Believer in an Age of Cranky Atheists* (Nashville: Thomas Nelson, 2012), 82.

4. J. P. Moreland, *Love Your God With All Your Mind* (Colorado Springs: NavPress, 1997), 132.

5. Douglas Groothuis, "Jesus: Philosopher and Apologist," *Christian Research Journal* 25, No. 2 (2002): 28–31, 47–52, www.equip.org/articles/jesus-philosopher -and-apologist/.

6. Lewis explicitly chronicles his intellectual journey to Christianity in *Surprised by Joy* and includes autobiographical allusions to his story in much of his fiction, including *The Great Divorce*. Among the writers and friends that influenced his decision, Lewis cites Plato, MacDonald, Herbert, Barfield, Tolkien, and Dyson (*Surprised by Joy* [London: Fount, 1977], 180).

7. Kreeft and Tacelli, *Handbook of Christian Apologetics,* 21.

8. Groothuis, *Christian Apologetics*, 29.

9. Ibid., 49.

10. Ibid., 49–50.

11. Ibid., 49.

12. This term refers to Rudyard Kipling's book *Just So Stories*, which offers extraordinary accounts of various phenomenon, such as "How the Whale Got His Throat" and "How the Leopard Got Its Spots."

13. Koukl, *Tactics,* 62.

14. Groothuis, *Christian Apologetics,* 52ff.

Chapter 10: Christianity and Pagan Myths

1. "Atheists Squander Nativity Scene Spaces at Santa Monica's Palisades Park," laist.com, Dec. 10, 2011, http://laist.com/2011/12/10/religious_protest_at_palisades _park.php.

2. Rene Girard, "Are the Gospels Mythical?" *First Things*, April 1996, www .firstthings.com/article/2007/10/002-are-the-gospels-mythical-11.

3. Derek Murphy, *Jesus Potter Harry Christ: The Fascinating Parallels Between the World's Most Popular Literary Characters* (Portland, OR: Holy Blasphemy, 2011), Kindle locations, 3358–3361.

4. In this book, *pagan* will be used to refer to those who are neither Jewish nor Christian. Nothing demeaning is intended by the use of this term.

5. David Marshall, *Jesus and the Religions of Man* (Seattle, WA: Kuai Mu Press, 2000), 9.

6. Ibid.

7. Cyclopædia, art. "Atonement" (abridged). Quoted in John Henry Newman, *An Essay in Aid of a Grammar of Assent* (Notre Dame, IN: University of Notre Dame Press, 1992), 392–393.

8. Ibid., 393.

9. Mircea Eliade, *The Sacred and the Profane: The Nature of Religion* (Orlando, FL: Harcourt, 1987), 130.

10. See also Jean Daniélou, *God and the Ways of Knowing* (San Francisco: Ignatius, 2003), 19.

11. Marshall, *Jesus and the Religions of Man,* 10. Here Marshall is referencing Mahatma Gandhi, Martin Luther King Jr., Benigno Aquino Jr., Nelson Mandela, and Aleksandr Solzhenitsyn.

12. Fulton Sheen, *Philosophy of Religion: The Impact of Modern Knowledge on Religion* (New York: Appleton-Century-Crofts, Inc., 1948), 215.

13. Robert M. Price, *Jesus Is Dead* (Cranford, NJ: American Atheist Press, 2007), 279.

14. Ross Douthat used this phrase on the April 20, 2012 episode of the HBO series *Real Time with Bill Maher,* www.hbo.com/real-time-with-bill-maher/episodes/0/245-episode/synopsis/quotes.html#/real-time-with-bill-maher/episodes/0/245-episode/index.html.

15. This is affirmed by *Nostra Aetate*, Vatican II's "Declaration of the Relation of the Church to Non-Christian Religions":

> Men look to their different religions for an answer to the unsolved riddles of human existence. The problems that weigh heavily on the hearts of men are the same today as in the ages past. What is man? What is the meaning and purpose of life? What is upright behavior, and what is sinful? Where does suffering originate, and what end does it serve? How can genuine happiness be found? What happens at death? What is judgment? What reward follows death? And finally, what is the ultimate mystery, beyond human explanation, which embraces our entire existence, from which we take our origin and toward which we tend?
>
> Throughout history even to the present day, there is found among different peoples a certain awareness of a hidden power, which lies behind the course of nature and the events of human life. At times there is present even a recognition of a supreme being or still more, of a Father. This awareness and recognition results in a way of life that is imbued with a deep religious sense. The religions which are found in more advanced civilizations endeavor by way of well-defined concepts and exact language to answer these questions.

(*Nostra Aetate* 2 in *Vatican Council II: The Conciliar and Post Conciliar Documents* [Northport, NY: Costello Publishing Company, 2004], 738.)

16. *He Is There and He Is Not Silent* is the title of one of Schaeffer's books (Carol Stream, IL: Tyndale, 1972).

17. Gerald McDermott, *God's Rivals: Why Has God Allowed Different Religions? Insights From the Bible and the Early Church* (Downers Grove, IL: InterVarsity Press Academic, 2007), 31.

18. McDermott seems to think that El Elyon is a Canaanite deity, which would imply more of a general source of revelation for Melchizedek. On the other hand, Scott Hahn and others, including St. Thomas Aquinas and Luther, suggest that Melchizedek is actually Noah's son Shem, which would indicate that he had firsthand experience with special revelation. See Scott Hahn, *Ignatius Catholic Study Bible: New Testament* (San Francisco: Ignatius, 2010), 425.

19. Don Richardson tells this story and provides the ancient references in *Eternity in Their Hearts: Startling Evidence of Belief in the One True God in Hundreds of Cultures Throughout the World* (Ventura, CA: Regal, 2005), 14–28.

20. That is why *Nostra Aetate* 2, in *Vatican Council II*, states that the Church "rejects nothing of what is true and holy in [pagan] religions" (739). It notes that, in their attempt to answer life's biggest questions, other religions have recognized a supreme being and tried to live accordingly.

21. Christensen, *C. S. Lewis on Scripture*, 52.

22. Ibid., 54.

23. C. S. Lewis, *God in the Dock*, 43.

24. *Nostra Aetate* 2, in *Vatican Council II*, 739.

25. Sheen, *Philosophy of Religion*, 241.

26. C. S. Lewis, *Weight of Glory (Collected Letters of C. S. Lewis)* (New York: HarperCollins, 2001), 128–129.

27. Jean Daniélou, "Christianity and the Non-Christian Religions" in *Introduction to the Great Religions* (Notre Dame, IN: Fides Publishers, 1964), 24.

28. Karl Rahner, "Experiences of a Catholic Theologian" in *The Cambridge Companion to Karl Rahner*, eds. D. Marmion and M. E. Hines (Cambridge, UK: Cambridge University Press, 2005), 301.

29. Pope John Paul II speaks along these lines in answering the question of why there are so many religions in *Crossing the Threshold of Hope* (New York: Alfred A. Knopf, 2006), 80–81. He refers to *Nostra Aetate* in noting that people turn to various religions to answer life's biggest questions, but all "have one ultimate destiny, God, whose providence, goodness, and plan for salvation extend to all" and that even as the Church can affirm the "semina Verbi (seeds of the Word) present in all religions" and a "common eschatological root present in all religions," the "Church is guided by the faith that God the Creator wants to save all humankind in Christ Jesus, the only mediator between God and man, inasmuch as He is the Redeemer of all humankind."

30. Daniélou, "Christianity and the Non-Christian Religions," 25.

31. George Bradford Caird, *Principalities and Powers: A Study in Pauline Theology* (Oxford, England: Clarendon, 1956), vii.

Chapter 11: The World Is Not Enough

1. A term popularized by Douglas Copeland in his 1991 book *Generation X: Tales for an Accelerated Culture*. It refers to the generation born after the World War II baby boom, generally from the early 1960s to early 1980s.

2. Ilya Shapiro, "Is That All There Is?" *TCS Daily*, April 19, 2005, www.ideas inactiontv.com/tcs_daily/2005/04/is-that-all-there-is.html.

3. Gregg Easterbrook, *The Progress Paradox: How Life Gets Better While People Feel Worse* (New York: Random House, 2004), xiii-xiv.

4. Ibid., xv.

5. See Charles Colson and Harold Fickett, *The Good Life: Seeking Purpose, Meaning, and Truth in Your Life* (Carol Stream, IL: Tyndale, 2005), chapters 22–24, for good discussions of conscience and other knowledge of God that is available to everyone.

6. Henry and Richard Blackaby and Claude King, *Experiencing God* (Nashville: B&H Publishing Group, 2008), Kindle location, 95.

7. Charles H. Kraft, *Christianity with Power: Your Worldview and Your Experience of the Supernatural* (Eugene, OR: Wipf & Stock Publishers, 1989), 39.

8. Groothuis, *Christian Apologetics*, 367.

9. Aldous Huxley, quoted in Huston Smith, *The World's Religions* (New York: HarperCollins, 2009), 19.

10. Eric Metaxas offered these excellent thoughts on leisure on the May 23, 2012 episode of *Breakpoint*. (Transcript available at www.breakpoint.org/bp commentaries/entry/13/19424):

For most people, "leisure" is synonymous with inactivity. It's what we experience when we aren't "doing something." Since we think of leisure as being passive, it makes sense that we fill our "leisure time" with passive entertainments.

But that's not how Christianity understands leisure. In his book *Leisure: The Basis of Culture,* the Catholic philosopher Josef Pieper called leisure a "condition of the soul." It's not the same thing as inactivity or quiet. It is "the disposition of receptive understanding, of contemplative beholding, and immersion—in the real."

Leisure, he writes, consists of "a celebratory, approving, lingering gaze of the inner eye on the reality of creation." It's about seeing the world as God made it, affirming its goodness, and thus transcending the hum-drum and cares of our everyday existence.

According to Pieper, "Only someone who has lost the spiritual power to be at leisure can be bored."

That doesn't mean that entertainment is bad *per se*. The problem, as Naughton says, is that "leisure understood only in terms of entertainment lacks meaning that is satisfactory to the human heart and mind." It can't satisfy us no matter how much of it we shove down our gullet.

Thus, we should ask ourselves *why* we watch a certain TV show or visit a certain website. Is it to relax or unwind, or is it because we are restless and afraid of being still or, even worse, afraid of the Real?

11. Blaise Pascal, *Pensees* 133/169, ed. and trans. Alban Krailsheimer (New York: Penguin, 1966), 66.

12. Kreeft and Tacelli, *Handbook of Christian Apologetics*, 80.

13. William Lane Craig, *Reasonable Faith: Christian Truth and Apologetics* (Wheaton, IL: Crossway, 2008), Kindle locations, 1388–1392.

14. C. S. Lewis, *Mere Christianity* (New York: HarperCollins, 2001), 50.

15. Ibid.

16. Kreeft, *The God Who Loves You*, 89.

17. St. Augustine, *Confessions* (New York: Penguin Books, 1961), 21.

18. Alcorn, *Heaven,* 160.

19. Kreeft, *The God Who Loves You,* 89.

20. St. Augustine, *Confessions,* 170.

21. Kreeft and Tacelli, *Handbook of Christian Apologetics,* 78.

22. Lewis, *Mere Christianity,* 136.

23. C. S. Lewis, *Weight of Glory,* 32–33.

24. Jean-Paul Sartre, "Existentialism Is a Humanism," a lecture given in 1946, in Walter Kaufman, ed., *Existentialism from Dostoyevsky to Sartre* (Amsterdam: Meridian Publishing Company, 1989), reproduced at www.marxists.org/reference /archive/sartre/works/exist/sartre.htm.

25. Al Gore, "Moving Beyond Kyoto," *New York Times,* July 1, 2007, www.nytimes .com/2007/07/01/opinion/01gore.html?_r=1&ei=5090&en=b53eb681db2b0e17 &ex=1340942400&partner=rssuserland&emc=rss&pagewanted=all.

26. William Lane Craig, *Reasonable Faith,* Kindle locations, 1531–1535.

27. *The Discourses of Epictetus* iii.24.2.

28. For an interesting example of this principle, see Nancy Sherman, "A Crack in the Stoic's Armor" on the *New York Times* Opinionator Blog, May 30, 2010. She interviews soldiers who used Stoic principles to survive war. However, as one veteran explained, at some point it's time to get back in touch with your emotions: "I've been sucking it up for 25 years, and I'm tired of it." Article available at http://opinionator.blogs.nytimes.com/2010/05/30/a-crack-in-the-stoic-armor/?hp.

Chapter 12: Up Close and Personal With God

1. Mo Willems, *Edwina: The Dinosaur Who Didn't Know She Was Extinct* (New York: Hyperion Books, 2006).

2. Christian Smith, *American Evangelicalism: Embattled and Thriving* (Chicago: University of Chicago Press, 1998), 173.

3. J. P. Moreland and Klaus Issler, *In Search of a Confident Faith: Overcoming Barriers to Trusting in God* (Downers Grove, IL: InterVarsity Press Books, 2008), 136.

4. Ibid.

5. Holly Pivec, "Exorcising Our Demons," Biola Connections (Winter 2006): 10–17, available at http://magazine.biola.edu/article/06-winter/exorcising-our-demons/.

6. For more in this area, see such thinkers as Francis Schaeffer, Chuck Colson, Richard John Neuhaus, and Nancy Pearcey.

7. Pivec, "Exorcising Our Demons."

8. Moreland and Issler, *In Search of a Confident Faith,* 155.

9. That is not to say that overtly physical manifestations of the demonic are the main way demons work or that we should focus on having "power encounters" with them. They usually operate (at least in the materialistic West) in much more subtle ways, such as lying and temptation. Neil T. Anderson, one of evangelicalism's most well-known spiritual warfare authorities, is a veteran of many overt experiences with demons, but, as noted in the Pivec article referenced above, he won't usually talk about these episodes, because he doesn't want to detract from the more common and primary demonic tactics of deception.

10. Groothuis, *Christian Apologetics,* 365.

11. This is not to say that all experiences must be authenticated by witnesses. Personal and interior experiences of the "numinous," for example, as described by Rudolph Otto in his classic work *The Idea of the Holy* (New York: Oxford University Press, 1950) are perfectly valid evidences for God. Also, the witness of the Holy Spirit in a person's life is valid and self-authenticating evidence for the truth of Christianity. However, I think you are going to have a much harder time talking to a skeptic about these types of evidences.

12. Moreland and Issler, *In Search of a Confident Faith,* 140.

13. Blackaby and King, *Experiencing God,* 170.

14. Michael Novak, *No One Sees God: The Dark Night of Atheists and Believers* (New York: Doubleday, 2008), 96.

15. Augustine, *Confessions,* 177–178.

16. God's use of miracles is given far too little attention in Western Christian evangelism. Craig S. Keener has done his part to remedy that situation with *Miracles: The Credibility of the New Testament Accounts* (Grand Rapids, MI: Baker Academic, 2011). I highly recommend this important two-volume work.

17. See Teresa of Avila's *Interior Castle* (New York: Image Books, 2004) for just one of many classic examples.

18. I've heard eyewitness testimony of this phenomenon from friends I trust.

19. Joel Rosenberg, *Inside the Revolution: How the Followers of Jihad, Jefferson and Jesus Are Battling to Dominate the Middle East and Transform the World* (Carol Stream, Il.: Tyndale, 2009), 387.

20. *Deadliest Catch*, Season 8. This episode, titled "Release the Beast," originally aired July 17, 2012.

21. Trevor Freeze, "A Story of God's Protection in Joplin," Billy Graham Evangelistic Association, June 16, 2011, www.billygraham.org/articlepage.asp ?articleid=7967.

22. James S. Spiegel, *The Making of an Atheist: How Immorality Leads to Unbelief* (Chicago: Moody, 2010), 26–27.

23. I don't have chapters in this book on evil and suffering, primarily because there are so many good resources already available. For a nice short summary, see Peter Kreeft, "The Problem of Evil" at www.peterkreeft.com/topics/evil.htm.

24. William P. Alston, *Perceiving God: The Epistemology of Religious Experience* (Ithaca, NY: Cornell University Press, 1991), 306.

25. Ibid.

26. Friedrich Nietzsche, *The Gay Science: With a Prelude in German Rhymes and an Appendix of Songs* (New York: Cambridge University Press, 2001), 157 (Section 277).

27. *The Gay Science,* in which this passage appears, also contains Nietzsche's first use of the term *God is dead* (Section 108) and the famous parable of the madman (Section 125), in which a "crazy" man warns the townspeople about the harsh consequences they can expect now that they have "killed" God.

28. For a good commentary on this passage, see Paul S. Loeb, "Suicide, Meaning and Redemption" in Manuel Dries, ed., *Nietzsche on Time and History* (New York: Walter de Gruyter, 2008) available at http://ups.academia.edu/PaulLoeb/ Papers/823236/Suicide_Meaning_and_Redemption.

29. Nietzsche, *The Gay Science*, 157.

30. Moreland and Issler, *In Search of a Confident Faith*, 143.

Chapter 13: Hypocrisy, Sex, and Other Causes of Skepticism

1. Frank Turek, "Sleeping With Your Girlfriend," Townhall.com, March 2, 2009, http://townhall.com/columnists/frankturek/2009/03/02/sleeping_with_your_girlfriend/page/full/.

2. Edward Feser, "The Road from Atheism" Edward Feser's blog, July 17, 2012, http://edwardfeser.blogspot.com/2012/07/road-from-atheism.html.

3. Kevin Vost, *From Atheism to Catholicism: How Scientists and Philosophers Led Me to the Truth* (Huntington, IN: Our Sunday Visitor Publishing, 2010).

4. Feser, "The Road from Atheism."

5. Lewis recounts his conversion story in *Surprised by Joy: The Shape of My Early Life* (Orlando, FL: Harcourt, 1955).

6. C. S. Lewis, *The Screwtape Letters & Screwtape Proposes a Toast* (New York: The Macmillan Company, 1967), 11–12.

7. Vost, *From Atheism to Catholicism,* 185.

8. John W. Loftus, *Why I Became an Atheist: A Former Preacher Rejects Christianity* (Amherst, NY: Prometheus, 2008), Kindle locations, 436–439.

9. Harris, *Letter to a Christian Nation,* vii.

10. *Gaudium et Spes* 19, *Vatican Council II,* 918.

11. Loftus, *Why I Became an Atheist,* Kindle location, 454.

12. James S. Spiegel, *Hypocrisy: Moral Fraud and Other Vices* (Grand Rapids, MI: Baker, 1999).

13. Russell Baker, *Growing Up* (New York: Congdon and Weed, 1982), 61.

14. Elizabeth Landau, "Anger at God Common, Even Among Atheists," *CNN Health*, The Chart Blog, January 1, 2011, http://thechart.blogs.cnn.com/2011/01/01/anger-at-god-common-even-among-atheists/.

15. Paul Vitz, *Faith of the Fatherless: The Psychology of Atheism* (Dallas, TX: Spence Publishing, 1999).

16. Spiegel, *The Making of an Atheist,* 68–69.

17. Vitz, *Faith of the Fatherless,* 16.

18. Elizabeth Stuart, "Fatherless America? A third of children now live without their dad," *Deseret News*, May 22, 2011, www.deseretnews.com/article/700137767/Fatherless-America-A-third-of-children-now-live-without-dad.html?pg=all.

19. Vitz, *Faith of the Fatherless,* 130.

20. Ibid., 134.

21. Ibid., 135.

22. Ibid.

23. Michael Shermer, speaking in *Nine Conversations: A Question of God,* a PBS documentary. Transcript available at www.pbs.org/wgbh/questionofgod/nineconv/transcend.html.

24. G. K. Chesterton, *What's Wrong With the World* (Public Domain Books), Kindle location, 405.

25. Vitz, *Faith of the Fatherless,* 136–137.

26. Mortimer Adler, *Philosopher at Large* (New York: Macmillan, 1977), 316.

27. Karol Wojtyla, *Love and Responsibility* (San Francisco: Ignatius, 1993), 143.

28. Brant Hansen, "The Big Objection: Our Culture, the Bible, and Sex," Air 1 Radio, Dec. 7, 2011, www.air1.com/blog/brant/post/2011/12/07/The-Big-Objection-Our-Culture-the-Bible-and-Sex.aspx.

29. When I refer to *nature* and *natural* in this section, I am using the terms in the classical, scholastic sense. That is to say, I believe creation and everything in it has a nature and is intended to live according to that nature, although sometimes it does not. As a result, not everything that occurs in the universe is "natural." Eyes that do not see are not operating "naturally" in the classical sense, for example. They are not fulfilling their purpose by operating according to their inherent nature. This is an important distinction to understand when talking to skeptics, because they will often use the term *natural* to refer to anything that happens under the sun. For example: "Humans have a desire for unrestricted sexual license, therefore it is natural." That is not the way I am defining the term.

30. G. K. Chesterton, "Ecclesiastes." This poem is available at http://www.poemhunter.com/poem/ecclesiastes-2/.

31. Aldous Huxley, *Ends and Means* (London: Chatto and Windus, 1941), 270–273.

32. Spiegel, *The Making of an Atheist*, 72.

33. Paul Johnson, *Intellectuals* (New York: Harper Perennial, 2007).

34. E. Michael Jones, *Degenerate Moderns: Modernity as Rationalized Sexual Behavior* (San Francisco: Ignatius, 1993).

35. Spiegel, *The Making of an Atheist*, 70–80.

36. I understand that the meaning of sex certainly does not seem obvious to many in our culture. However, that only shows the extent to which we have gone to suppress the truth. Part of my argument in this section is that sexual immorality is so egregious precisely because it involves refusing to accept truth that is so plain and clear. It's like God is shouting in our ear with a megaphone while standing in front of a huge neon billboard, yet we ignore him. That is not to say that all of the subtleties of sexual theology will be obvious to all, but the basics are not hard to discern. For example, the idea that men and women are made for each other and that procreation is inextricable from this relationship is a truth every culture in the history of the world until ours has accepted without debate.

37. There is more to abortion than just sexual sin, of course, but the primary motive for abortion is a desire for sexual license. Arguments about personhood and the health of the mother, etc., are basically all a smoke screen to hide the plain desire of pro-abortion advocates to have another form of birth control. I write more about this on my blog at donjohnsonministries.org. Just select the "abortion" category.

38. John Paul II, *Original Unity of Man and Woman: Catechesis on the Book of Genesis* (Boston: Daughters of St. Paul, 1981), 114 (From the January 16, 1980 lecture).

39. Matthew Lee Anderson, *Earthen Vessels: Why Our Bodies Matter to Our Faith* (Minneapolis: Bethany House, 2011), 125.

40. Dietrich von Hildebrand, *Purity: The Mystery of Christian Sexuality* (Steubenville, OH: Franciscan University Press, 1989), 7.

41. Anderson, *Earthen Vessels,* 127.

42. The thoughts in this section are taken primarily from a series of weekly lectures Pope John Paul II gave in 1979 and 1980. These lectures are known as his "Theology of the Body" and are available in several forms. The communion of persons referenced here is from the November 14, 1979 address: John Paul II, *Original Unity of Man and Woman: Catechesis on the Book of Genesis* (Boston: Daughters of St. Paul, 1981), 70.

43. Peter Kreeft, *Everything You Ever Wanted to Know about Heaven—But Never Dreamed of Asking* (San Francisco: Ignatius, 1990), excerpted at www .peterkreeft.com/topics/sex-in-heaven.htm.

44. Feser, *The Last Superstition,* 224.

Chapter 14: Telling the World Its Story

1. Vincent Miceli writes that atheists make "what seems like a valid appeal to the reason of their fellowman. In reality, however, upon closer analysis this appeal to reason is seen to be counterfeit; it is nothing more than a massive propaganda assault upon the mind intended to swamp the light of reason with its intensive passion. Not the compelling force of evidence, but the compulsive force of passion pressed into the service of half truths and downright falsehoods is ceaselessly employed to fashion conformity and unanimity of mind in favor of atheism" (Vincent P. Miceli, *The Gods of Atheism* [Harrison, NY: Roman Catholic Books, 1971], 460).

2. Richard John Neuhaus, "Telling the World Its Own Story," Catholic Education Resource Center, www.catholiceducation.org/articles/apologetics/ap0081 .html.

3. Ibid.

Donald J. Johnson is the president of Don Johnson Evangelistic Ministries. He has served in vocational ministry since 1993, including extensive work as an inner-city missionary and pastor of young adults. He has a BA in Theology, Missions, and Intercultural Studies from San Jose Christian College (now William Jessup University), an MA in Christian Apologetics from Biola University, and an MA in Theology from Franciscan University of Steubenville. Don and his wife have four children and live in southern California.